# Burning My Roti

## Breaking Barriers as a Queer Indian Woman

**Sharan Dhaliwal**

*Hardie Grant*

BOOKS

Illustrator: Aleesha Nandhra
Design Director: Lisa Rahman

# PREFACE

This book examines our brown bodies against a scale of whiteness. It's not an easy read for some – I discuss body disorders, racialised and queer histories, anti-blackness and self-hatred. This isn't a self-help book. It won't tell you how to improve your life 'in just three easy steps!' and it definitely won't leave you feeling a sense of gratitude for the world. If anything, it exists to help us understand why we live in a constant state of inadequacy with ourselves. It's an acknowledgement that this is a shared experience.

The book is laden with the uncomfortable word 'white'. 'Whiteness, white supremacy, white privilege'.

Still to this day, there's a sense of fear in talking about whiteness – although I don't discuss it only as a skin colour but as the proximity to power. For example, Priti Patel (South Asian Conservative Home Secretary) has strong Karen energy. She enforces white supremacist ideals in the way she governs. You don't have to be white to be ... white.

There are also words in this book that some people may not understand, and while it's common practice to italicise or explain a word in brackets when it's from a different language, my intention is not to do that. I remember hearing Nikesh Shukla once speak on this and he said he hoped for the day when our words are no longer italicised, and I agree with the sentiment. While some people may not understand these terms, there are many words I've come across in a book that I've had to Google. So, Google them. (But for the sake of accessibility to privileges such as Google, I have added a glossary at the back.)

Through a retelling of lived experiences (some ridiculous, some traumatic), I delve into my relation to whiteness: as a

light skinned, thin, cis Punjabi woman, juxtaposed against my mental health, eating disorders, hairy body and the expectations of someone with a womb. While I am not susceptible to many forms of discrimination, I can look at it critically while removing myself from it.

We're told to love ourselves first, but self-love and radicalisation can be violent when women of colour have to love themselves, despite themselves. And the overarching forces of patriarchy that play a leading role in this.

We've all felt inadequate in our lives, whether it's from our job, relationships, friendships or mental health but when we look deeper, patriarchal structures are the columns holding these values inside us. While such values are powerful, there's a sense that as easily as they are built, they can be torn down.

We have rules which we must abide by in order to reach fulfilment and of course these rules are important. We have to observe certain laws to keep an order. We aren't creatures that have predetermined structures in our system – our bodies are susceptible to disease and our periods sync with someone we stand in a queue with for too long at the post office. There's chaos in our inherent existence, and so chaos will ensue outside it.

While a structure has been created for us to live inside, the laws and rules within it are created by us: the very chaotic beings we are attempting to control. As these rules have developed through trial and error, so have we. Technology has advanced us, philosophy has enlightened us, and history has taught us. Scratch that. It *should* have.

The problem is, we exist in a world that possesses the power to eliminate anything due to inconvenience.

Whether it be a forest, an immigrant or that person's feelings – we have not grown in compassion, but in selfishness. So where does the analysis of humankind leave us with this book? That lack of selfishness is what has led to our current societal norms – these norms are what we expect. We don't dare imagine turning on the TV to find, for example, a Black lesbian feminist leading 'the free world'. That's not our expectation. We turn on the TV and a racist old man with ideologies that pre-date any enlightenment tells us an insensitive joke about people who aren't white. This is the norm.

We are told to survive a crushing expectation that is thrust onto us since birth and every breath from our squashed lungs is a victory. Although the victory may seem small and pointless, it's about being alive in the middle of this. As I write this, I look outside, and the world is tearing itself apart. Climate change has decimated Earth, a global pandemic has sent death and shockwaves across the globe, Black people are killed at alarming rates, Muslims are pushed in front of trains after an islamophobic attack and inequality has proven to be a huge factor in the high death rate for people of colour. These implications of supremacy have existed before we were born, before our parents and their parents. They existed from the discovery of power.

With this power comes great ... no, I'm not going to quote Uncle Ben from *Spider-Man*.

The point? This power and responsibility lie on the shoulders of men. The men who make decisions to structure us, our lives, our bodies, our intentions. We aren't free thinking, free willing – we are within the boundaries of what

has been set up for us. But the thing with power is that it can been passed around and abused by almost anyone. So, why can't we take the reins of our own existence?

An intersection with ethnicity is vital – from immigration or colonisation – the governing of our bodies against whiteness is what sets white women and women of colour apart. In Western countries, the pinnacle of beauty is aligned with the cis-gendered women that appeal to them specifically, so in European and American (after invasion) countries it tends to be thin white women with soft features and large breasts. In India, a country which has been colonised, there is such a strong need to strive for a particular Western beauty, that skin lightening creams are their largest selling beauty product. This crown of beauty is ever-changing with an acceptance and appreciation of different body types – yet taking on 'fads' to monetise off the norm is another form of colonisation.

White people have accepted some forms of body shapes, as long as they can also adhere to them. What has happened is the autonomy of our bodies is still left in the hands of another.

In 2016, I founded the magazine *Burnt Roti*, which I called 'a platform by South Asians, about South Asians', and it became the driving force behind my activism. Its success was cemented around conversations about plastic surgery and body hair, which brought in our biggest audience. It eventually branched out to discuss sexuality, mental health and identity – which also has a strong connection to how we perceive our beauty. My article 'Being A Hairy Indian' is still to this day, the most read article on the website.

There's a strange relationship formed between freedom

and trauma when discussing health, sexual and race-based identity issues. This became evident in the way *Burnt Roti* functioned – while giving a voice to people, it was still difficult to sit in our truths. I guess this book has the same feeling. I want to discuss a lot of topics, but at the same time, it has brought up a lot of trauma and uncomfortable truths. Writing this book isn't cathartic, in fact it fuels more anger. Not towards myself and my decisions, but to the world that continues to perpetuate these ideals on young women and non-binary people of colour.

Sweeping generalisations don't help people here, so let me be specific – while I talk about the forceful and established censorship of women of colour's existence, it's coming from my experience to talk specifically about Indian women. And through that, we have an open dialogue here of colonial influence, anti-blackness, ethnic cleansing with plastic surgery and existing simply for the male gaze. While we are conditioned to be the carrier of children, the incubators of the seed – we are much more than that. While we ourselves are born into this patriarchal world with every agency to live as we are; as soon as we begin to live, we're told we're doing it wrong. Actions are scrutinised for not being 'ladylike', which translates to 'how will you find a husband?' These norms have become our life lessons, with the food we cook, the way we speak and the clothes we wear.

But what if you aren't here to satisfy a man? What if you're here to merely exist, just like them. What if you want to satisfy a woman? When your sexual identity comes into play, this conditioning becomes distinguishable. We're at a tug of war with rich white men and they keep winning, but their strength is dwindling, and something has to finally give way.

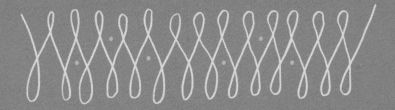

# CONTENTS

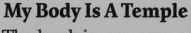

# 1

# iDENTiTiES

Duelling identities

● dentity is hard defined. Are we governed by who we love, the amount of melanin in our skin, the languages we speak or our ancestral lineage? Or all of the above? A lot of people find certain terminology gives us space to exist, almost as a safety net but others find it restricting. Am I a bisexual British Indian woman? What if I want to identify as queer instead? And do I really consider myself British in any way other than where I happen to have been born? 'Indian' is my lineage and 'woman' is my gender which I have not rejected, although an implication lives inside me to reject all gender binaries for a more fluid existence. So, even 'woman' feels restrictive now? All that's left is 'Indian', yet I still can't write in Punjabi and although I understand it completely, I can only speak it moderately. I don't know whether these boxes exist for me to tick to be considered Indian, but I'm not sure what else would. My mother and father were both born in Punjab, and their parents before them and so on. Maybe that's it. Then there must be a disconnect somewhere, because I was born in England.
The British Indian. The queer British Indian woman.

   My parents emigrated to the UK in the 70s, settling in Southall, also known as 'Little India'. It was primarily known as a hub for immigrants from South Asia – British soldiers from India opened factories around the Middlesex area and hired Indians to work in them. The close proximity to Heathrow and its bustling job market also helped with the influx of South Asians settling in. Soon Southall became a bedrock for South Asians, (predominately Sikh people), to live respectfully and celebrate their culture. A 2011 census

Identites

revealed that in Southall, 76.1 per cent were Asian, 9.6 per cent Black and 7.5 per cent white. Southall Broadway had the lowest proportion of white British residents of anywhere in the UK – 93.7 per cent of Southall Broadway's population were Black, Asian and minority ethnic.

I grew up there and in Hounslow, another predominately South Asian and immigrant area, which interestingly defined a lot of my apprehensions about my identity. While I did fall into some stereotypes (I did watch Bollywood and eat Indian food), I fell outside of it a lot of the time. And so, my credentials felt inadequate but the fact that I felt like I needed credentials shines a light onto the essence of my uncomfortable journey with myself.

When I lived in Southall, it was after protests and riots had occupied the town. In fact, I hadn't yet been born. In 1976, white skinheads taunted and eventually killed 18-year-old Gurdip Singh Chaggar, on a night out with friends, which resulted in the largest youth-led organising of protests and riots that Southall had ever seen, resulting in further arrests and deaths. The Southall Youth Movement (SYM) was formed, where thousands of South Asian, Black and white allies stood up to the police and the National Front (a far-right political party who are known for inciting hate and violence from their racial populist and neo-Nazi beliefs).

But when I lived there, I was unaware of this; I learned about Southall's history years later. I was privileged to not feel too outcast for my skin tone due to the accessibility I had to Asian-ness. Although, with this comes different layers of issues, through enforced cultural preconceptions

# 'I sometimes wonder whether I had the need to identify myself to make others comfortable with my presence.'

on how I should 'turn out' from the people I was surrounded by. Being born a queer person was definitely not what they had envisaged. Any conversation around sexuality was non-existent, so I found myself constricted to only understanding my future through the eyes of others. I was either marriage material, or I was a lost cause, but there was no in between. For me, the in between was discovering myself and accepting that life would lead me down a different and more intriguing path. A path that I was interested in, instead of the tiresome idea of being married to a man just to pop out a series of kids.

I came out by publishing an article in my magazine Burnt Roti, without telling anyone I was doing it. It took me a whole 20 minutes to write and a whole 30 minutes to hover over the publish button before pressing 'send' and throwing my laptop across the room. The response was an outpouring of love. But I also had comments from people in the surrounding area who were too apprehensive about revealing their sexual identity. It became clear that it wasn't just my experience, but that of many queer people that grew up in a largely immigrant area.

Sexuality was used as the butt of a joke: 'he's acting gay!' someone would say while laughing at a character on TV. Leaving us feeling belittled in a lifestyle that can so easily be mocked. There was little conversation, sure, but I also wondered what the conversation could have looked like. When I was asked by a company to help translate some videos to Hindi and Punjabi, I realised the lack of accepted language around certain terminology. Now, these videos were about sex toys and sexuality, so there were many uncomfortable moments when I had to text my mother phrases for translations: 'how do you say 'it felt weird on my ...'' censoring the word 'clit' from my message.

While words existed for 'lesbian' and 'homosexual', they were not used often enough for people to truly recognise them. It turned out a lot of English words substituted terminology for homosexuality and sexual acts, because of the influence of the British Raj. It meant I was unable to identify my sexuality within my own culture.

I sometimes wonder whether I felt the need to identify myself in order to make others comfortable with my presence. If white British people were able to define my existence, they could understand why I was there – why I was on that land. But the ambiguity and lack of education around global ethnicities means the onus is on us to come up with a definition and put ourselves neatly into a box.

So, I kept trying to figure this out, and have been at a battle with understanding my identity and in fact, the need to understand it. This led to *Burnt Roti* curating an exhibition in 2016, called 'The Beauty of Being British Asian' or 'BOBBA' for short. It was Burnt Roti's first exhibition, and I was interested in showcasing the artists I had discovered through my magazine. After reading an essay submitted by writer Nikita Marwaha, I envisioned each line with a piece of artwork beside it. This visual interpretation of the essay was so strong, I couldn't shake the feeling that it had to happen. Lines such as 'It's opening a tub of ice cream in the fridge and being faced with frozen daal ... It's feeling like a foreigner in India and looking like one in the UK', were so striking that I could see art accompanying it. So, I sent a call out to artists, including the ones I had already discovered to be part of this exhibition and not long after, I had a group of amazing people who were excited about being part of the discussion.

The idea was to represent, but the risk was I would only be scratching the surface, and that would be deemed the acceptable level of commentary – in other words, we don't want the uncomfortable details. I continued invalidating those who felt unseen, including myself. Not to say others weren't represented, they definitely were and so were those who took part in the exhibition. It was valuable on many levels, especially to the queue of people waiting outside to enter all saying, 'we have nowhere else to go to feel this seen'. And that's beautiful. But I found myself questioning the line between identity and art. While art has always been important to me, I felt that the way in which I was consuming it moulded my identity, and in turn my inability to truly showcase myself.

# Interview with Zarina Muhammad from The White Pube

I've spoken to Zarina Muhammad about the dynamics of identity, Britishness, Asian-ness (all the ness's), a few times but wanted to delve into it more for this book. She co-runs The White Pube alongside Gabrielle de la Puente, which is a platform where they both look critically at the art world as two people who aren't 'boring white men'.

'**D**iaspora art feels tied to a cycle of dealing with the condition of duality that the diasporic body rests in', Zarina says in an article she interviewed me for in 2018, called 'The Problem with Diaspora Art'. Diaspora art is defined by Zarina as 'art made in diaspora about the diaspora, as a flattened condition that operates aesthetically'.

I called her up to discuss this further. The thing about 'diaspora art' is much of it takes a particular form: where images of South Asian people are juxtaposed against Western themes. But why are those two so important to connect in art?

'Diaspora art is part of a way more complex web of institutional trajectories – these labels exist to assimilate whiteness, as a component, into how we construct and handle our identity. It's about reacting to that white gaze.'

The main point here is that there is institutional racism within the art industry, which allows PoC (people of colour) to exist only for the institute's comfort and desire. I wondered whether BOBBA was perpetuating that racial comfort. I went to an art university, although I barely paid attention, was very drunk and was more concerned about who I wanted to date or sleep with, over achieving any qualification. I didn't work on building my critical eye when it came to observing art, so despite wanting to work as a curator, I wasn't as equipped as I would like to have been to deliver a representative exhibition. And potentially, because of this, didn't critically ponder the comfort of diaspora art to whiteness. So, I then questioned if my knowledge of art and identity as a British Asian woman was limited to what's been shown to me through racist art institutes.

Zarina continues: 'To equitably host PoC within itself, it will have to completely disassemble that entire racist structure and reorganise itself on

completely different logic. Instead of doing that it transplants people into it, and they fill the spaces that already exist. Institutions are microcosms of societies at large – it replicates those structures and amplifies them.'

That placement of a PoC into an institute to create art, almost like a plaster on top of their racism, is indicative of how society holds PoC to account. So where does aesthetic-based diaspora art sit within this? We dissected this the best we could, although the critique of diaspora art can be difficult because of an inability to separate self from art. Without critiquing the person, it is difficult to critique their art. Zarina explains it to me as: 'art is created, then it lives in a

space and then it makes a social, cultural or political reference, or in a sense has an awareness of it.'

'The reason diaspora art flops', Zarina ties this point together well here, 'is because it doesn't do those next steps, beyond making the artwork. It doesn't do anything when it comes to the conceptual unpacking or that critical attention between an artwork's mode of display and exchange, and the social, political, cultural – all those remain empty, so the institution is able to instrumentalise the artwork and the artist next to the artwork. By flattening identity into the art, the artist is required to be part and parcel of the artwork, and so it only makes sense in relation to the artist.'

We both realise how this sounds, and it becomes a sticking point that we find ourselves in too often. I confess to Zarina that I stream Zayn's (Zayn Malik)

music when it comes out, but I don't actually enjoy it. I do it for the culture. But what is really stopping me from being able to critique something within my culture? Is it because the space is usually taken by white people, and I don't want to stand beside them?

'I'm down for the culture, I'd ride for it, but the way diaspora art works, it's purely representative and my role as a critic is to provide feedback to the artist, audience and institution. In terms of the feedback for the artist, you can step away from your work and it can live a life away from you and we can talk about this critically – that's part of the conceptual education, you need to talk about it away from yourself. It just needs these improvements.'

Zarina pauses.

'Maybe that actually is a super European relationship to have with an artwork actually, because it treats it like an intellectual exercise and for diaspora art a lot of the time it's an expression of self and it is hard to disentangle self from the conceptualisation of the artwork.'

So, is diaspora art working within the confines of a racist institution – is that why it doesn't quite hit the nerve on identity? We have no answers, don't expect answers in this book.

She ends with: 'There's no escape, art is a bourgeois activity – fine art as a practical category emerged from a bourgeois service for the aristocracy, it's hard to peel away from that and have it become something that exists for the masses, and so this conversation becomes what role class has and how we function in terms of it.'

Unfortunately Zarina's full quote on the matter wasn't used because she already clearly expressed her point, but I also wanted to mention that she referred to the UK as a 'piss island' and I cackled for an uncomfortably long time.•

**Z**arina and I finished our discussion by focusing on identity through diaspora art and how we align ourselves to it. We wondered what came first – the lifestyle or the art. But I have never worn a sari with ripped jeans, because although I am both Indian and British, I don't see what combining these two things would do for my 'identity'. Although I have worn Indian jewellery with Western clothes in order to give a sense of living with both identities, like a statement. But in my mind, it always felt forced – I wasn't doing it because I genuinely have this jewellery sitting on my dresser, waiting to be worn – I had to fish it out and be like 'yeah, look at this white people: I'm Indian'. Why I couldn't just wear jewellery for the sake of jewellery being worn, was telling of my need to identify with ... well, something. Which box was I sitting in and for the comfort of whom?

The good thing about boxes is they can be broken down; the flimsy cardboard can tear and rip as we grow too big for it. While changing attitudes around immigrants and histories are being taught at schools, we are in control of how we are defined. The problem here is what we consume can be filtered through a racial lens in art, so while we see ourselves one way, we are still told we are only acceptable as the other.

But the acceptable is still a stereotype. There are barely any South Asian women I know who fall in line with the 'demure' and 'subservient' stereotype. I know a lot of South Asian queer, non-binary and trans people. I know South Asian goths, mothers, change makers, activists, sex workers, gamers, musicians and the list can go on and on forever. There is no box to keep us all in.

And this is not to discard any part of ourselves that we want to identify with. I still say British Indian, no matter how at odds I am with it. My Indian ancestry is deeply important to me – more important than being born on British land. My queerness is important to me and so is my acceptance of my body: the body they tried to rip from my hands, with their own definition. As I stand at a tug of war, one end yelling 'a mother' and the other yelling 'my choice', I realise that I'm at a tug of war with myself.

Moments for revelations are unceasing; you don't come to one moment in your life and consider everything

resolved. We're ever-changing with the climate we live under, and so our relationship with our identity changes alongside it. Nothing is set in stone, so we may consider ourselves disconnected one day and the next, we may be all we ever needed.

Immigration was started off the back of colonising lands and the slave trade, so has always had negative connotations, which have been made to look pretty with sentiments of 'improving one's life chances'. Now, it's about ethnic minorities (or in the lead up to the Brexit referendum, EU citizens) in Britain stealing jobs and indulging in the country's benefit system. It no longer relays any positive feelings onto those who hear it. And usually those who are attempting immigration have to deal with a hostile, racist and xenophobic system set up to essentially keep immigrants out of the country. From Trump's Muslim ban to the UK's point-based system, there is no open-door policy that would make anyone feel welcomed. And the strange concept of borders is based on commodities and power struggles – from the need to import/export, while protecting natural resources, to the power-hungry cis-hetero-patriarchal men who govern land. But outside of this, there is no real reason to stop others from gaining access to different lands.

It's definitely a lot more complicated than this, with various dense political textbooks with inane regulations that fill up all the gaps which have led us here, but in the mind of those without that knowledge (like me), the word 'immigration' has certain connotations. Some think of migration as a burden, and people like myself may relate

'We're ever-changing with the climate we live under, and so our relationship with our identity changes alongside it.'

it to trauma. Trauma can be acknowledged from forced migration witnessed in history, and the biggest form of this is the transatlantic slave trade.

Forced migration is the result of war, natural disasters and displacement – causing populations to move to safer surroundings. In some cases, it means being expelled due to one's ethnic, religious or cultural beliefs. A lot of the time, the reasons behind communities migrating across the world aren't to steal your job, but in fact find safety. The uncomfortable truths are that when powerful people use migration for their own benefit (slavery, colonisation, occupying land), it isn't considered a problem. However, when people from poorer countries, who have different cultural backgrounds, move for the hope of a better or safer life, they are considered a burden.

The feeling of being a burden is ingrained in many immigrants, after movement. My family moved here and knew they weren't British unless they assimilated in a way that kept them close to whiteness.

This whiteness that I will talk about in this book, isn't just about the colour of skin, but the proximity to power, wealth and systems that benefit a select group of people, because whiteness isn't only white people, but from people of all cultures. Whiteness is the power that leads us to believe we're not good enough. It's the ultimate goal we're told to achieve. While there are some white people who do not benefit from whiteness as much as others, they still have a closer proximity due to their skin colour. These dynamics are hard to define, because we're in a multi-cultural society that achieves economic growth through things like immigration – those people stealing your jobs are actually keeping your country afloat. I suppose, whether they are achieving closer proximity to whiteness is not explicitly known; what is true is that they are striving for it.

Some examples of trying to achieve whiteness could be adopting accents, anglicising non-English names to sound more English or simply adhering to power structures of capitalism and consumerism. Am I saying my family were striving to achieve a whiteness that could benefit them? Absolutely. And I think that many people are doing this, whether they know or not. Myself included.

Identities

# Interview *with* Dad

I spoke to my dad about
his immigration experience.
It was interesting, because
the older generation
don't speak about their
experiences, either so they
can assimilate easier or not
to regurgitate trauma.
It can be difficult for them
to remember moments that
were harmful; a lot of
the time they dig it deep
inside themselves.

When speaking to Vinay Patel about his play *An Adventure* about immigration and love, he told me it was based on his family's experience. I was fascinated to find out how he managed to prise out the story from his family – every time I try to ask mine about their past, they brush it off with a joke or change the topic. In an interview with *Burnt Roti*, Vinay told me: 'A few years after my maternal grandmother passed away, I bought a tape recorder and fifty odd tapes for my grandfather and asked him to record stories from his life on it. Just a little, every morning ideally, but if he didn't feel like that was fine too. I wanted to give him a project, something to distract him, and whilst he has insisted that we don't get to listen to those tapes until after he's died, he started to open up a little more in casual conversation too.'

I loved that concept and have spent a while speaking to my dad about different intersects of life, and one day I managed a phone call where he told me details about his experience. 'I was Kuldip Singh until the passport people asked which village I was from and I said Dhaliwal, so they wrote that down', he told me over the phone. 'I was given one at the passport office. Nobody used surnames in India.'

I didn't know that. My surname was given to my dad when he immigrated. He didn't like that concept, and so when my brother was born, he was given just 'Singh' as his and mine stayed as Dhaliwal: 'the intention was that yours would change after marriage.' He laughed looking back at that thought.

I asked about my name 'Sharan', as it's very white sounding and I was aware that my mum actually wanted to name me 'Shweta.'

'I knew it would be easier for British people to say your name if it was Sharan. I had to deal with people not being able to say Kuldip Singh – they all eventually called me KC (K Singh, to KC) and it was frustrating.'

He came to the UK in 1967 on a family sponsorship visa at the age of 16. I was curious

about what his feelings were about England when he reached there at such a young age.

'There was a keen anticipation, I had read Shakespeare and Dickens and wanted to experience the worlds that they created. It was because of the historical education I had, which was colonialised because of the schooling me and my friends had. Normal schooling was teaching Hindi, mine was still teaching how great colonialism was. We were brainwashed into thinking Britain was great. Then I came here. I had to sweep floors and when I was told to "get a move on" by the boss who didn't think I was doing it fast enough, I felt so disgusted in myself.'

That was hard to hear. But it got worse.

'At work, I had to find somebody to be around me (because I was very skinny) who didn't get beaten up by white people. I maintained that cover for a long time. You had to give supervisors part of your wages to get a little bit of protection as well.' He mutters something under his breath I didn't quite hear but I can imagine it was a response to a traumatic recollection of that life. He takes a deep breath and continues.

'Getting on the bus going to work, you had to avoid people shouting at you all the time. They shouted. "Get away from there." You couldn't sit next to a white man. You had to stand. If ever I went to a pub with somebody, there was a separate section for people of colour. You couldn't go to the other side and if you did, to play darts or whatever, you were taken outside and beaten up. We didn't have an identity, we were treated like dogs.'

The hostile environment created by immigration policies and the hostility of the environment you're then introduced into isn't as easily fixed by being a so-called 'good immigrant.' You can code-switch all you wish, but there may still be violence enacted on your very being.

'I changed myself: bought myself a motorbike, grew my hair long – if they wanted to call me a hippy, let them. I was in a gang for a short period, and from there decided that wasn't for me and that's when I became part of college culture.'

The power of white supremacy was more obvious in the 60s and 70s. It works insidiously now, although a lot of the time it's focused violently, it also does so quietly. Through

micro-aggressions that chip away at your being on a daily basis. I don't mention to my dad about the racial abuse I've received because I didn't want to 1) belittle his everyday experience with sparse stories from me and 2) make him think that the pain he faced was for nothing. Because a lot of the older generation feel like the worst is over. That they experienced it so we don't have to.

Saying that, racism isn't quantifiable. We can't sit there and tally up stories to see who has experienced the most. It reduces the impact and ignores our history.

'I was your classic example of a coconut. I thought I should have been accepted because I wasn't your "run-of-the-mill Indian", I thought I would have been at a better position at work, by being able to speak English and dressing like them, but there were no opportunities', he continues. I know in many ways the landscape has changed and that through more work, it will continue to change. The underlying problem here, though, is the structures that have been built that we're working on changing. If they are fundamentally racist, would adding our voices to that racism help or make them louder?

Through labour, my dad found better jobs, made his way into the world of work that benefitted him and allowed him to settle into the British life. This career progression is well known in many immigrant families – you start in a factory, eventually get into an office job and then one day you become a manager of sorts. He made money, bought a house and finally, he was considered British enough. •

Identities

While these systems exist all around the world, we can't say that being an avid consumer makes you a white supremacist, but there is a clear connection between capitalism and racism. I still go wild at discount codes for brands that don't need any of my money. I still guilt buy when I'm feeling depressed. I definitely try to buy from independent PoC-owned businesses, but I still buy most of my shoes from Adidas. What we can do is try to consume fairly, inside the margin of access we have. But either way, money itself and any form of exchange benefit a consumerist and therefore white supremacist society.

So you're probably at the stage where you're thinking to yourself: 'why, for the love of god, does she keep aligning everything to white supremacy?' and if you're white, you may be saying 'I did nothing wrong!!!'

First, unfurrow that brow and relax that ass. Whiteness is also known as the illusion of power and it infers to the access to power – this is within and outside of skin colour. Asians have a proximity to whiteness closer than a Black person, and so can inhabit white supremacy.

Now, white supremacy as an overriding power system is the nature of capitalism: the governing of society through wealth. This is held in the hands of white people (hence 'white' supremacy), and before your ass stops relaxing – the concept is held globally through the routes of capitalism. So yeah, it's not just white countries that have unjust systems (I see you, Modi), but it's the inherent concept of whiteness that becomes the system.

I think the point I'm trying to relay here is that we can't blame each other for the way we have lived our lives, when the real villain is the systems set up by white elitist men. While my intention to create an exhibition that represents 'British Asians' may have fallen short, the institutions of art have led me to that stage. While my dad immigrated in the 60s and came across racial abuse, so will I. Although a racist cis-hetero-patriarchal society exists for me to inhabit, it's difficult to escape it and live comfortably. And no matter how hard I try to define my identity, there will always be a system in place that disregards it in some form.

Identites

'You couldn't
sit next to
a white man.
You had to
stand.'

# Let's talk about sexual identity, baby.

'I'm bisexual' I announce to the world.
'Oh yeah? Name three ex-girlfriends', the world replies.
'Um ... I mean I don't have that many ...'
The world giggles and turns its back to me. I'm reminded of being back at school – I was the least popular girl, bullied for having a large nose and facial hair. Now I'm talking to people within and outside of the LGBTQ+ community and wondering where I belong.

To me, it all seems connected – my journey with my nose, body and facial hair, and especially my battle with my identity. I went to a predominately Asian school and felt I wasn't Asian enough, because maybe I wouldn't get married to a man. And while I battled with that, I listened to everyone in my school talk about their crushes, and joined in, squashing any hopes I had for other genders. I wasn't sure if I was allowed to have a crush on someone other than on a boy, but I already knew boys wouldn't like me back because I didn't fit into the beauty standards that would lead me to be desirable. So ... a double whammy of self-doubt.

It's not to say that all Asian people at that time talked about getting married or that their successes were all defined by having a family, but it was an underlying understanding in a lot of households. So, this transmitted into everyday actions – from how you presented yourself, to the people you became friends with. A lot of pressure comes from expectations to continue your ancestry for economical and family values. The saying that money makes the world go around wasn't plucked out of nowhere – it truly impacts each element of your life. It is a big part of the injustice and racism faced by people, exacerbated and a lot of the time governed by wealth inequality. It affects your physical and mental health and your decisions in taking action are born from this. Money can't bring you happiness, but poverty causes death.

And money is important here – when talking specifically about Indian weddings, words like 'dowry' are mentioned. You show off with gifts, jewellery and parties. Parents have worked, suffered and saved, solely to get you married and make it look good. So, if you spend a lot of your childhood wondering if marriage is even for you, you're telling your parents that everything they've done since they gave birth to you is pointless. Obviously, that's ridiculous. But there's a lot of truth in the way some traditional families perceive your

Pictured above: *Bend it Like Beckham* (2002)

actions, and often, they try and persuade you with guilt.

I found myself questioning why gender affects this potential path. Whether I marry a man, woman or non-binary person – does it matter, as long as I continue economic growth and carry the family name? How naive of me.

We need to remember that legally, it was assumed that it was only economically beneficial to marry someone from the opposite gender. Legislation hadn't passed to allow same sex marriage in the UK until 2013 and up till then, there was no financial and legal rights given to same sex couples. Meaning, being able to have what was considered a 'successful' life was but a lost dream. An assumption was also made that it wouldn't be taken seriously, they wouldn't have children and divorce rates would increase. Whereas in reality, the coupling of two people benefits the state through large weddings, pooling of savings and gaining large assets. The commodity of marriage doesn't judge. Interpersonally, there's a chance you're going to have a divorce or decide not to have children, no matter if you're gay or straight.

Homosexuality was considered a 'Western' concept. Although, it wasn't until the British colonised India and hence criminalised homosexuality, was it to be illegal.

Of course, we're not saying that everyone lived in a happy utopia, but it wasn't part of the law. Maybe it's a form of trying to appease the English, who 'saved' the Indians from 'savagery' (thanks Churchill?), or maybe it's a genuine misunderstanding – but a lot of Indian families I know who immigrated to England from India, were and continue to perpetuate homophobia.

# History of Section 377 Timeline

## 1861

The British brought
in Section 377,
criminalising
homosexuality.

## 2009

They were successful
and homosexuality was
decriminalised.

## 1991

The act was repealed in
a report called *Less than
Gay: A Citizen's Report*.

## 2013

The Supreme Court
reinstated Section 377.

## 2017

It was reviewed
by the High Court.

## 2001

The NAZ Foundation
filed a petition
to repeal Section 377.

## 2018

Homosexuality was
finally decriminalised
(again) in India.

**THE DETAILS:**
In 1861, when the British Raj had colonised India, they brought in Section 377. It was modelled on the Buggery Act of 1533, which made sexual activities 'against the order of nature' illegal, including homosexuality.

In 1991, AIDS Bhedbhav Virodhi Andolan (the first AIDS/HIV activist group in India) asked for its repeal in their publication *Less than Gay: A Citizens' Report*.

In 2001 the NAZ Foundation revived this. This non-governmental organisation, who also worked in the field of HIV/AIDS intervention and prevention, filed a petition declaring that Section 377 – in penalising sexual private acts between consenting adults – violates the Indian Constitution.

In 2009, they were successful and in the case Naz Foundation v. Govt. of NCT of Delhi, the Delhi Court's two member bench agreed that it violated human rights and decriminalised homosexuality in a landmark case.

In 2013, the Supreme Court's two member bench (Justices G. S. Singhvi and S. J. Mukhopadhaya) overturned the decision of the Delhi High Court, in the case Suresh Kumar Koushal v. Naz Foundation, saying the 2009 and reinstated Section 377.

In 2017 it was reviewed by the High Court, after several petitions and in the case Navtej Singh Johar v. Union of India.

In 2018, homosexuality was decriminalised in India. Two of the lawyers involved in this case were Arundhati Katju and Menaka Guruswamy – they had filed a petition winning the landmark case.

I t was in 1861, when the British Raj had colonised India that they introduced Section 377. Modelled on the Buggery Act of 1533, it sought to make sexual activities 'against the order of nature' illegal. It said: *377. Unnatural offences: Whoever voluntarily has carnal intercourse against the order of nature with any man, woman or animal, shall be punished with imprisonment for life, or with imprisonment of either description for a term which may extend to ten years, and shall also be liable to fine.*

It criminalised homosexual acts, non-consensual acts, bestiality and sex with minors. What that meant is that anyone who was caught acting on their orientation through sexual activity would be imprisoned, while simultaneously aligning homosexuality with bestiality and paedophilia. There were a few court proceedings before 2018. In 1991, AIDS Bhedbhav Virodhi Andolan (the first AIDS/HIV activist group in India) asked for its repeal in their publication *Less than Gay: A Citizens' Report* and was revived in 2001 by the NAZ Foundation. This non-governmental organisation, who also worked in the field of HIV/AIDS intervention and prevention, filed a petition declaring that Section 377 – in penalising sexual private acts between consenting adults – violates the Indian Constitution.

The parts of the Indian Constitution they pointed to included the following Articles: 14 (equality before the law), 15 (non-discrimination), 19 (freedom of speech and movement) and 21 (right to life and personal liberty). What the NAZ Foundation revealed was that the homophobic elements of this Section, which was still in law, violated numerous human rights and therefore had to be scrapped. They were successful and in the 2009 case Naz Foundation v. Govt. of NCT of Delhi, the Delhi Court's two-member bench agreed that it violated human rights and decriminalised homosexuality in a landmark case.

A few years later, in 2013, the Supreme Court's two-member bench (Justices G. S. Singhvi and S. J. Mukhopadhaya) overturned the decision of the Delhi High Court, in the case Suresh Kumar Koushal v. Naz Foundation, saying the 2009 order of the High Court is 'constitutionally unsustainable as only Parliament can change a law, not courts.'

They reinstated Section 377.

Then it changed again, and this is where we are. When it was revisited in 2017 by the High Court, after several petitions and in the case Navtej Singh Johar v. Union of India, homosexuality was finally decriminalised in India by 2018. Two of the lawyers involved in this case were Arundhati Katju and Menaka Guruswamy, who recently came out as a couple, revealing the true meaning of 'power couple'. They filed a petition and represented lead petitioners in the case, winning the landmark case. In an interview on CNN, Guruswamy spoke about the re-decriminalisation in 2013, '[it] was a loss as lawyers, a loss as citizens. It was a personal loss ... it is not nice to be a 'criminal' who has to go back to court as a lawyer to argue other cases'. Arundhati added: 'We had a court where we practised as lawyers and this court had just told us that gay people were second class citizens'. When discussing the new ruling with Columbia Law School, Guruswamy said 'It's a wonderful day,' while celebrating the ruling with fellow lawyers. 'We are thrilled with the decision because the court has gone much farther than decriminalisation'. She was commenting on their appeal to love and life, and even the Court's apology for past mistreatment. The time, the energy ... the journey is exhausting and it's a stark reminder on how judicial systems work. But there's still so much work to be done.

Interestingly, in India's history, it has been considered to be a far worse criminal offence for women to have sex out of marriage than for two men to have intercourse. The punishments were also reflective of this – in *Same-Sex Love in India: Readings from Literature and History* written by Ruth Vanita and Saleem Kidwai. It was noted that women who had sex outside of marriage would incur a fine, whereas the charge of homosexual intercourse between men would be withdrawn by 'eating the five products of the cow and keeping a one-night fast'.

Ancient Hindu texts have depictions of homosexuality throughout them – in *Tritiya-Prakriti: People of the Third Sex: Understanding Homosexuality, Transgender Identity and Intersex Conditions Through Hinduism*, the author Amara Das Wilhelm looks into the reason behind the changing attitudes from ancient India to modern day and notes that 'society has only recently begun to understand sexual orientation, gender identity and intersex conditions, and our legal and social systems are just beginning to catch up with and accommodate such people in a fair and realistic way'. So, while we have fluidity within us, it's the systems that we created that are yet to catch up with our natural states.

This fluidity is evident with the existence of the Hijra community – they have a recorded history of over 4,000 years. The Hijra people are queer, trans and/or intersex people who are recognised as a third gender. They have featured in the Kamasutra, as well as ancient Hindu texts such as the Mahabharata and the *Ramayana*. The idea of a third gender has existed for longer than we can imagine in many cultures and having only two binary genders is in fact a modern creation. During the Mughal era in India, many people from the Hijra community held positions of power in politics, and were considered to hold religious authority, particularly during religious ceremonies. It was under the British rule that the Hijra community were criminalised, through various laws, with the plan to completely eradicate them.

In modern days, they tend to perform at weddings and similar celebrations, where they are paid to sing and dance and interestingly, even though this can seem like exploitation (in some ways it can be), they are revered during religious occasions. Despite this, they are still discriminated against, through verbal and physical abuse. Their social status is still suffering, through housing issues, inaccessibility to healthcare and discrimination in education and employment.

It was in 2009 when India officially recognised trans and intersex people as a third gender, eligible for welfare and other government benefits. It highlighted more issues within the community, where they still had problems voting and were still heavily discriminated against.

With this history, someone could assume that it may not be that difficult being a queer Indian woman, yet through the ideals forced on us from the British Raj and the ongoing battle queer people have for their basic rights, there's still a lot of uneasiness around it. And, as always there's still an expectation for women to marry men for servitude.

But it wasn't until I felt comfortable enough to question the norms forced on me, that I began to live life as myself – as a queer Indian woman, with the ability to fall in love with whoever I choose.

Yet I find myself gritting my teeth through the word 'comfortable', because I'm not sure how much comfort is afforded to me. I felt unsure about my own sexuality, because the reality was I was supposed to be with a man. It wasn't about what I desired. That led me to wonder if I had rejected these expectations so much that I had believed I was queer in order to further rebel. I had convinced myself that maybe

Identites

'I was conditioned from childhood to get married to a *"good man from India"* and it was ingrained so deeply in me that I didn't realise I was also being conditioned to be straight.'

it's not true that I want to be with someone from any gender.

As I just wrote that, I see how ridiculous it is. I see that now.

But why wouldn't I feel that way? Why wouldn't I be on edge about the realities of my existence, when my whole life it was being written out for me?

I always wondered if people could see something in me that I was unaware of. Was I oozing queerness? 'Lesbian' was an insult, followed by 'slut' and 'churail' (witch) – all said to me when describing people who were 'bad' or 'unnatural'. I trusted adults, so I believed them. And now, as an adult, I don't know whether to believe myself.

It's not individual people I look to blame when I feel this pain, it's the system that was built to make them believe it to be true – people enforce a lifestyle that they know works. It's not their fault, but it's unfair that they have not been able to unlearn these behaviours before pushing them into the lives of their children and grandchildren.

When I fall in love with someone other than a cis man, the first thing that pops into my mind is 'what will they do to me?' Not in a fear of physical violence but violence isn't always shown through a slap across the face, it can also be through shaming and disconnecting. While some of my families are liberal enough to not care, there were many I feared would not want to see or speak to me again.

The fear came alongside stubbornness, because if they don't want to talk to me because of who I love, then I don't want them in my life.

'In the way they judge me,
I will judge them right back.'

# Radical self-love

I had to learn to love being myself. I wasn't sure how it was done – whether empowerment is achieved from merely recognising your insecurities, or if facing them was a literal practice. If the literal practice was acts of breathing and aligning my 'chakras', then it was achievable right? As I tried to examine the concept of self-love, I found it was practised predominately by white people, somehow colonising and changing ideas of wellness to suit their individual needs. For example, in meditation, the idea of breathing out bad thoughts and breathing in new ones is a westernised concept. In Buddhism, you must breathe in the bad thoughts and take them in, because the path to reach wellness is to be selfless.

Yoga is a regularly discussed colonised practice, although I don't practise it because it tends to inhibit sexual desire, whereas Kama, a very similar form of stretching, does the opposite. Basically, I'm too horny for yoga. But we see a lot of yoga classes taught by white people, who use a westernised form to benefit their western life. Taking a practice and using it for your needs is a great idea and there would be nothing wrong with that if they called it something else, stopped lighting incense during their classes and refrained from saying 'namaste', which by the way tends to mean 'hello' in most conversational situations.

I wasn't sure whether to mention all this, because I'm not here to tell you what is already known. We know that yoga is colonised. What I want to discuss is the difference for PoC practising wellness in a westernised country, with a westernised form of their original motherland. Let me try and make that sentence make more sense …

I was discussing wellness with another Indian friend of mine and how we are told to 'do yoga' or 'meditate' when activism becomes traumatic. And because we are westernised beings, born and brought up in the UK, we would, or should even, practise these versions of wellness. But our route to wellness is different. Our experience of wellness is different. While our minds are able to connect in a similar way, our history, which sits deep inside us, does not connect with these practices as easily. We came to the conclusion that wellness was different for different people.

'So, if white people are the ideals of beauty, they also became the ideals of wellness, no matter who they took the practice from.'

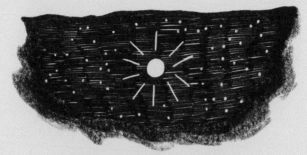

# Interview *with* Kallie Schut

To understand the concept of decolonising wellness practices, I spoke to Kallie Schut – a British born yoga teacher of Indian heritage. She works to bring cultural awareness to the practice and develop everyone's understanding of the colonial legacy in modern yoga. It's a conversation that I don't see enough yoga teachers having, especially from those who aren't South Asian.

**I** have a Sikh Punjabi background, my parents migrated to England in the early 60s, from former colonised lands. They moved to Birmingham, to Smethwick and moved to Marshall Street – in 1965, that street was the scene of race riots. White people who lived in the houses on that street, didn't want the houses sold from the council to people of colour. They were campaigning, putting up racist slogans on their windows, skinheads marched down the street breaking windows and throwing petrol bombs, which all preceded the Rivers of Blood speech by Enoch Powell. So, it was a really racially hostile environment that my parents arrived in. So right from the start, I was born and lived on that street for the first 18 years of my life.'

This is important to know when we discuss the harm in communities of colour who migrate, especially when discussing generations of trauma. Kallie grew up with yoga practised in the house, and even took part in it herself. She was taught aspects of Sikh and Hindu practices, celebrating both. I remember that my upbringing was very similar – I would get taken to a Sunday school, where we learnt about Hindu mythology. It wasn't until later, when Kallie witnessed yoga in the hands of whiteness, that it really affected her.

'As I became an adult and moved to London, I wanted to make friends so went to the local community centre and for the first time, I took part in a public yoga class. I also went to a gym's yoga class. Both of those experiences were awful, because I felt alienated. The moment I walked in, I felt unwelcomed (I was the only person of colour) and felt disempowered – I felt that somebody else was teaching me about my culture. They were the expert on something I had grown up with or something that I had seen brown people around me practising. They were mispronouncing stuff or not indicating that it had anything to do with India, I was like "what in heaven's name are they teaching people?", I thought it was wrong, and knew I had to fix this somehow.'

This led to Kallie's practice in decolonising yoga. With the way she grew up and the way that yoga made her feel when practised in public, she had to change the environment it was in.

'Yoga and wellness are a political subject, rather than a personal subject. These are wisdom traditions that were colonised and oppressed as part of the British rule in India. When they were lifted from India and imported into the West, they had gone through the process of colonisation. We know that yoga is rooted in dharmic traditions – Sikhism, Hinduism, Jainism, Buddhism – they are all part of the same family tree. Islam's Sufism also shaped yoga.[1] That has all been erased in the modern understanding of yoga in the West. For example, you either have a Hindu practice, or you have it as a sanitised, wellness, feel-good, self-development type practice. Both extremes fail to recognise that this is a story of people that have been marginalised and erased and written out of history.'

The uncomfortableness that Kallie felt in going to classes held by white people was the same feeling I had. I knew that yoga came from Indian traditions of practising wisdom, but I didn't understand the depths of it, until Kallie explained it further.

'Yoga and Ayurveda are both South Asian sciences – they are used for healing, restoration, for physical, mental, emotional and spiritual wellbeing. This is knowledge and wisdom held by our ancestors, discovered through centuries of Earth-based practices. So when they arrive in the West and have been commodified, commercialised and the capitalist structure of profit has been applied, it becomes a big money making industry. On the one hand, you have a minoritised, racialised culture of people who are disenfranchised and disempowered, those who have been subjected to a violent and brutal oppression historically, in their ancestral histories but also daily lived realities. And then you have this multimillion-pound industry, generating huge amounts of wealth for white people, mostly white women, who have completely stripped the practice of its roots and heritage of its tradition. That's where the harm is. Indians didn't invite the

[1] See reference Refractions of Islam in India: Situating Sufism and Yoga by Carl W. Ernst, SAGE YODA Press; First edition (22 Jun. 2016)

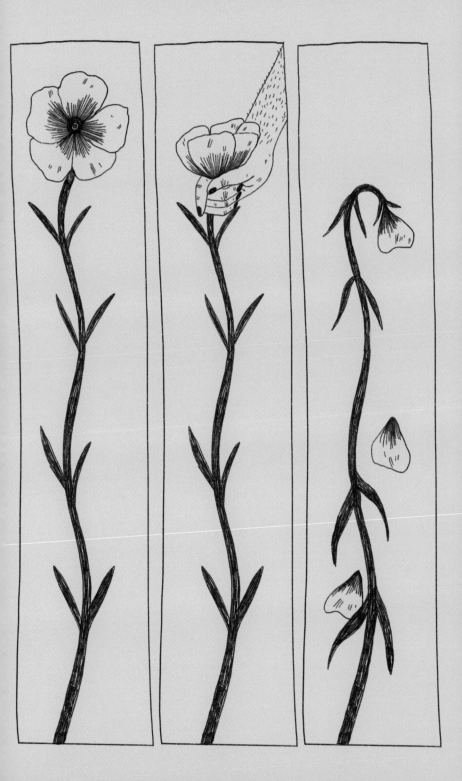

> 'Yoga and wellness is a political subject, rather than a personal subject. These are wisdom traditions that were colonised and oppressed as part of the British rule in India.'

British and ask them to come over, they extracted and exploited all the resource and wealth of people of colour and took away their identity. By stripping people of their identity, you can sub-humanise them, dehumanise them, and then you can oppress them. This practice about healing, recovery, spiritual enlightenment, working through the cycles of life and death, has been taken away from people of South Asian heritage and been sold as a commodity, as a packaged box with a pretty bow and some essential oils in it.'

This hit the nail on the head. I told Kallie how important her work is because even though some of us feel uncomfortable, we can't articulate why or how. Especially when it comes to an activist's radical self-love. 'Your self-care has to involve care for others.'

Kallie explains it further. 'As spiritual beings, we have a soul and in this embodied experience as a living person, our soul is working through all the things that have happened to us in our previous lifetimes. Dharmic traditions believe in reincarnation and that's the karmic cycle – birth, life, death, rebirth and so on. You keep going through those cycles until your soul has been able to shed all the chains and causes of suffering – until you are liberated. The purpose of yoga is so we can liberate the soul from this physical body and we return to the divine source, which could be God or universal consciousness. What we're doing in this lifetime is creating patterns of behaviour in which we do social good so that we change the life of others around us. We recognise our privileges and places of power and we recognise where there may be that intersectionality of oppression. By doing that, we can begin to liberate ourselves. This is the work of someone who believes in radical love and in sacred activism. That's what's radical about it. When you become selfish and it's about feeling good about yourself, being rested, with eye masks and massages – if that's where your care ends, and you never move into collective care, you are causing harm to others.'

The radical love we feel, is in our work and when I speak about that – when people tell me to take time for myself, for example – the time I take isn't solely for myself, but for others around me. Without bringing in that depth, I am simply harming those around me. By singling out my pain and concentrating solely on that, I am ignoring the world around me.

'My experience of walking into a yoga studio is the same experience of white violence, because it's coming from a place of ignorance, supremacy, white hierarchy, and occupation. The harm that is caused, is that not only has the practice been taken from us, but we are now not even allowed to be experts, be influencers, or teach knowledge in the practise itself, because the space is occupied by white-bodied people. It's cultural extraction and cultural exploitation. That is what my work is based on'. •

think about what has been taken from us and how we can attempt to reclaim it – either in the work Kallie is doing or in other forms of activism. The point here isn't to stop white people from doing yoga, because it's an incredible spiritual and political practice that people should all experience – the point here is that the history and connection it has with South Asian people should never be discarded. And the conception and movement from the motherland, into the hands of whiteness and capitalism, should not be ignored either. Understanding that and including it in your practice does two things – it allows you to truly benefit from the experience, and it also allows South Asian and other people of colour to feel welcomed in your practice.

This movement of wellness to the Western world means that the very act of wellness has changed from being a pure and simple practice to love yourself, to another moment of activism. While these are interconnected in many ways, it also drains significantly from the energy we are trying to maintain.

For me, and many others, self-love isn't about ourselves. In order to feel good, the world must feel good. So, while burnout, trauma and pain are experienced internally, it is also universal and ongoing. In order to feel some kind of balance, I believe that self-love is about loving others. That can be through any form – either by showing kindness or changing inequality for a community group. That can be done in youth work or workshops with young people, for example – either providing the knowledge or the space for it to happen. You don't have to be an educator to allow young people to learn about white privilege, you can

'The point here is that the history and connection it has with South Asian people should never be discarded.'

merely allow its teaching. We need to remember that telling someone they are loved and acknowledging them can fill you with joy and a reason for existing.

Pampering and gifting yourself is different. And I guess that's where the term 'self-love' can be discussed, because it isn't really about spirituality, but has been co-opted by the movement. Loving yourself is very different – it tends to be around moments of treasuring your existence by treating your body. These moments are important too and should be practised alongside any spirituality. I think I just have a problem with surface-level progress, whether it's with yourself or with others. They tend to be easy wins – momentary peace in chaos. But the chaos still ensues and you're still uncomfortably existing inside it. It's temporary because we can't find fulfilment in ourselves when those around us don't have it, and surface-level actions are a plaster on that wound. Soon the plaster will come off and the unjust world continues to burn around you.

I don't and won't deny the need to spend on our own to make ourselves feel better – although I believe we all need to find love by helping others, I also believe that it's difficult to do as someone who dislikes themselves. It just shouldn't end there.

Let's not forget that the colonisation of lands and then the theft of spirituality comes hand in hand when we look at perpetuated racism. These co-opted practices were taken during a white supremacist reign and so those ideals were transported with it. Caste systems were exacerbated, and culture was diminished. So, while we consider how a culture has been removed and restructured in yoga for example, it was done in violence and bigotry. The translation means that these practices in the West, now used by the very whiteness that took it, are also violent and bigoted.

If we look at astrology, we see something similar happening. Although prediction systems were global, many that are used now are developed from Indigenous lands. I may not be an expert on astrology, as someone who only sends people memes with 'me' and only recently figured out what my rising and moon signs are ... I have always known it to be something that exists in Indian culture and has for a very long time. Astrology can be traced so far back: there's evidence of Mayans and Mesopotamians using it as a prediction system back in BCE. And the Greek and Romans used them too – systems based on stars, Gods and planetary movements, amongst other things. But rarely do I see any nods to astrology's conceptions. Beyond memes, the movement of planets and its effect on our lives (through environmental, scientific and spiritual concepts), is created by Indigenous people.

I'm not saying that every time you say 'oh you're a Taurus, oh no', you have to recognise the history of astrology. It would just be interesting to see how people read it with the knowledge of how and when it was created. And especially why it was used – for example, because of the lack of scientific systems and technology, moments were predicted through observations and omens. From farming to political decisions, omens such as flight of birds or movements of planets would rule society.

Again, all these systems should be used by whoever wants to – the importance is in understanding the history, violence, the reason for the conception and then applying that to your practice. When we acknowledge the intersectionality of everything around us, including the trauma, then we truly benefit from these practices.

Identites

# Now make it queer

On top of it all, defining bisexuality became part of my personality; like a walking dictionary, that would open directly at the page containing 'bisexual', from being rigorously examined.

The effect of semantic satiation on 'bisexual' added to devaluing the experience – each time it's explained I lose a bit of love for it. The passion I initially felt when I came out dissipated into an unsatisfying relationship with myself. I found myself over-explaining my relationship history, until I realised ... I didn't need to explain it in detail.

People don't understand bisexuality – 'oh yeah, you're a lesbian now aren't you?', some joke half-heartedly, unable to even conjure enough energy to pretend it's a good line. I always laughed back – loudly and uncomfortably. I wonder if I even understand bisexuality.

A lot of these conversations and what tends to create self-doubt, is a focus on the act of sex itself. And that's the issue, because your sexuality is not defined by sexual acts.

When I came out, I wondered who I should prove my bisexuality with. Which woman should I obsess uncharacteristically over? I suddenly found myself becoming a devout romantic, following women on Instagram and liking way too many of their photos, wondering if that's a 'bisexual' amount of likes. Do they know I'm into women too? Is that enough likes? Is that too many? Who even is this woman? I'm actually not really into her at all. *gasp* I knew it. I'm not bisexual at all. I quickly post an image of Keanu Reeves and wonder if that's bisexual enough. Zoë Kravitz follows quickly after.

Balance.

I have experienced all these fascinating moments of questioning my own existence, to the point I wouldn't be surprised if it turned out I was a figment of David Lynch's imagination. I continue to question it and I probably forever will. Things that are taught to us in childhood manifest in trauma and our mental health. We are told to unlearn but we will not be able to forget. But I'm not the only one, and it's not just with bisexuals, or Asians. There is trauma in everyone, and self-doubt is part of our existence.

Coming out gave me something I didn't expect.

Queerness made me see myself through the lens of other queer people. And it was a radical act. The term 'queer' itself, shrouded in its history of being a slur, was defined as 'strange' and that was fascinating to me. Because to the world, the way I consider myself, is strange.

The LGBTQ+ community's very existence is considered as 'different' and so a lot of us live in what is perceived as 'radical'. Our bodies, which are originally controlled by the norm (cis white men), begins to blur into our own hands. You see a lot of the queer community working in the field of body and hair positivity, and that's because they have been othered to such an extent, that they have created their own ideals. And in terms of gender and sexual identity – they regularly open the world to concepts that define them. A lot of the time, the world isn't ready, with gender critical activists and TERFs (Trans-Exclusionary Radical Feminists) filling our timelines, newspaper columns and online social media news feeds – but the work is being done and has been for a long time.

Not to say this process is easy – it's come up against discrimination, criminalisation and abuse. Yet the existence of the conversation around bodies, identity and gender being in your hands, means that acceptance within the community becomes shared.

The history of radical queer self-love is rooted in queer people having to face rejection, bigotry and a high mortality rate. Community groups rise up during these times and wellness is a huge aspect to community health. So, self-love is tied into queer existence. When we aren't afforded the love, acceptance and rights to exist in this world, we have to create it ourselves. As RuPaul would say 'if you can't love yourself how in the hell you gonna love somebody else?' and that's the point here, because queer love and acceptance is passed within our community too. This can come in the form of having a chosen family, where we celebrate, support and elevate each other.

When we are told our bodies aren't good enough, we thrive within ourselves and our community, so self-love becomes an important part of existence. This is true within communities of colour too. When we are called names, told we're not good enough and are ostracised from society, we have to value ourselves in order to survive. This connection

Identities

'People don't need to know my past relationships, who my first crush was and when I first touched a woman. You can put your wagging tongue away and clean the spit off your chin.'

# 'But alongside the doubt, coming out opened a new door of queer self-love.'

between queer and non-white radical self-love creates a beautiful intersect, but at the same time it's a shame that it has had to happen the way it has.

The idea of a chosen family gives a sense of protection for people when they come out and could possibly lose their biological family. So, a connection is made with other queer people to love and protect each other. This is a creation of Black and brown, queer and trans people. From the ballroom scene to drag – a queer acceptance of self and each other (despite competition) is how we survive.

For queer PoC, the idea of 'wellness trends' transcends heavy breathing and yoga poses. It transcends the Headspace app. It is, unfortunately for a lot of us, a colonial and violent hang up. Maybe I sound frustrated and bitter, and maybe I am. It's not plucked out of thin air though; it came from lived experience and that should be examined.

The path of coming out, understanding my sexuality, taking care of myself, loving myself – it became a journey doused in more confusion. I still didn't feel comfortable, and I still didn't understand where I sat in the world. I think I came to realise I needed to stop looking for somewhere comfortable, because the discomfort of being who I am isn't mine, it's someone else's. The reason I feel strange, or 'queer' is because of the impact that others' perceptions have on me, instead of my own. Maybe instead of trying to reach wellness in my queerness through yoga, I would find it in my resolve to fight. And maybe my understanding of my sexuality was never meant to happen, because it isn't easily defined and definitely shouldn't be. I rarely call myself bisexual anymore, because I'm not sure how I will fit in that box. I think I don't want to fit inside a box. I think I just want to run around, fighting the good fight, while trying not to face too much violence. That's the dream.

I didn't know I was going to experience that. It reminded

me that my definition of beauty was formed by men and for men. When they're taken out of the equation ... well, we become freer.

This led to the creation of Middlesex Pride; an event that was meant to launch in 2020, but due to global pandemic, the first one took place in 2021. I was aware that growing up in Middlesex, where there was a lack of visibility of queer people, I felt unwelcome in the community and wasn't sure I was supposed to be in it. After coming out, I got hundreds of messages from people, but the messages that stuck the most, were from people who recognised that Middlesex was a reason behind their secrecy. 'I grew up in Hayes and saw no gay people, and especially gay Indian people, so I didn't think it was for me', a message that echoed in my mind a lot.

I realised that although my experiences were personal to me, many parts of it were shared within the community. Again. And again. This was a pattern I wouldn't stop seeing. Beyond the stereotypes of Bollywood or eating samosas with ketchup, there was so much more that we shared. I wanted to change that and so came up with Middlesex Pride. Not only is it difficult to travel to central London for Pride events (although it's always a nice escape to be freely queer), it can often be a daunting prospect. I wanted an event that people from the Middlesex and surrounding areas could attend and celebrate being themselves.

Middlesex needed a queer presence. Although there are some small pockets of gay bars or pubs, they were always hidden or shut down. It needed something that could be archived, used politically, and give residents the ability to access themselves. A pride event couldn't get closed down or kept secret. It's pretty loud.

The borough itself is a largely immigrant area and I realise that a lot of cultural and religious ideals are the reason behind the lack of queer visibility. In order to help people feel seen, there needs to be an open communication with these communities, so any preconceptions can be debunked. We hope that there's a future in Middlesex, where queer people will feel comfortable to exist freely in that space and not feel vulnerable.•

# 2

# THE HAIR CHRONICLES

My moustache
was thicker than his

Have you ever shaved your whole face and neck, and tried to shape your eyebrows with a razor, minutes before going to school, only to realise how obvious it is that you've just done that and everyone will notice and rip you to shreds but you can't stay home because your family know you're feeling fine and bunking off makes you nervous anyway? No? Just me? Cool.

That day was ... a lot. I was sweating heavily as I walked into the school building, feeling like all eyes were on me, but forgetting how invisible I was to many. The few would find me and continue their bullying, but this would be new ammunition. This would give them the energy they need to renew from their recent lacklustre heckles.

I wondered if I was overthinking, one of my favourite pastimes, but as I entered the home room, I heard it 'oh my god, look at her face', followed by cackles. I went bright red and did what I always did. I cried in the toilets.

My anxiety-ridden quick shave had left long hairs randomly sticking out of my face, lines of hair and then bare skin, and a rash on my neck. It wasn't the 'hot new look' I was hoping for. Not long before, I had a group of people from my school outside my house, yelling 'ugly' and 'man' at me, while I looked on from my window. It had driven a desire to make them happy. I wanted them to stop, but to also desire me. Shaving my face was a big part of that badly considered decision.

Before then, I used a hair bleaching cream called Jolen, where I would sing the classic 'Jolene' while applying it (but the Queen Adreena version because I was so metal) while it stung my sensitive skin. But I was aware of the orange and yellow hair on my brown skin.

'My femininity was questioned and as a child, I struggled with how to perceive my self-worth without it.'

'I wasn't looking for someone to tell me that it was okay to have facial hair, I was looking for someone to tell me it was beautiful. I wanted to be beautiful.'

I wasn't the only one, there were so many young Asian women in my school who had facial hair too. Yet, I declared myself the hairiest. Like an award I didn't want.

My femininity was questioned and as a child, I struggled with how to perceive my self-worth without it. I was taught that my femininity was what made me who I am. It constructed the very essence of my being, because it was tied to my sole function – to be admired enough to carry and birth a child.

Alas, a beard and moustache do not entice men, mostly because of the proximity to masculinity and homophobia precludes it. Toxic masculinity plays a big part in the construction of a young woman's self-worth and acceptance, as the cis-hetero-patriarchal system we are born into guides our every movement. From 'pink' and 'blue' colour-coded clothing to the gender pay gap – we are told we are different and inferior.

So, there's almost a want in some of us to reach the goals that aren't afforded to us. I had a beard, so I wanted to remove it in order to be beautiful enough for a man. Although, in doing so, I'm reaching the goals set by men, not myself. I was playing into their game, and despite knowing deep down that I probably didn't want to be with a man and carry his child, I still played.

I coveted white women on my TV who were presented as being hairless and confident, staring at their bright teeth shining from beyond a hairless, feminine face. I would open a magazine and see lipstick adverts, squinting to see if I could spot any moustache hairs from the heavily photoshopped image. By consuming manipulative mediums like TV, film, magazines and anything related to media and especially from the way it warps life in an unnatural way, I began to view my natural self in an unworthy light.

# Interview *with* Soofiya

I spoke to illustrator Soofiya about navigating body hair and facial hair through their lives and it was a really revealing conversation, mostly because not only did it echo a lot of what I went through, they opened different doors to ways of thinking. Soofiya is an artist who creates work about their identity and about their perception of themselves.

oofiya's admission that despite growing out their body and facial hair, they weren't always happy, was refreshing to hear. 'I have good days and bad days', they said and like any other person, that is true for every part of our lives. There are a lot of conversations around body hair positivity, where people talk about the joy in being yourself and being transparent, but they tend to avoid the trauma that comes with it. Because there ARE bad days. And these bad days make you question your very existence. 'Although I haven't grown out my facial hair and I remove a lot of body hair, when there are times that I don't, I mostly feel shame and there haven't been enough moments of joy alongside it.'

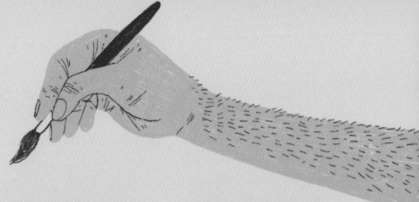

The conversation took a new turn, when Soofiya mentioned the history of hair being showcased in art: 'When did facial and body hair stop being painted?'. That's a really interesting point because the visual aspect of body hair is lacking, and our intake of art and beauty seems to come from hairless images. But we also know that hair removal is a modern and western tradition. So when did facial and body hair stopped at getting painted? And why?

'When you look at the Renaissance period for example... it's a colonised history so I'm expecting a lot of whiteness within it. But when you even think about the Mughal era illustrations – I don't see body hair in the depictions of feminine bodies. These kinds of gendered ideas are very clear cut, I guess the question is do we do not see them because the images were not saved or documented because history is recorded by the colonisers, the victors – so the dominant narrative is always well preserved compared to the marginalised narrative'.

It's true that our knowledge of history is recorded for us – unless we can find original transcripts or art from indigenous communities, it's sometimes hard to know how lives were actually lived. Especially when we're considering colonised lands.

'It's not to say hairy bodies didn't exist in art – they could have done, but they weren't preserved because there's only space to preserve the dominant narrative, anything that goes against that is easily lost intentionally or not'.

Soofiya noted that this lack of visual representation causes us to punish ourselves. They said that we live in a very punishing society with little accessibility to rehabilitation. When we should be rehabilitated, through furthering knowledge, we are instead punished for whatever unfair ideals have been forced upon us. And that comes through in our justice system where we see punishments forced onto those who are the most discriminated against in society.

Many people could consider any concern over beauty standards and body

ideals as narcissism, whereas these ideals which are forced on us and the perception that comes with it, is judgement and punishment. The punishment that we receive from this isn't just from society, but from ourselves. From the way we violently remove hair to the way we side eye someone for not removing a visible moustache. Remember, it isn't just something 'to get over', because we see it everywhere. And when we don't adhere to it, we're othered.

A lot of Soofiya's art is of their self: 'I think there's value in people drawing bodies that don't look like theirs and in the ways we communicate visually, particularly in opening up to visibly marginalised bodies', they ponder, 'the thing is, maybe this body/hairiness/ self can only be appreciated in a disconnected form, in the context of art – maybe it can only really be seen in a contrived and controlled space because it's not allowed to exist in public, without reason or cause.'

In art and the media, hairy bodies are celebrated – through photos on Instagram and exhibitions, we see all body types drawn, posed and observed. But in real life? 'I've never walked out the house and not been harassed – these are the two big disconnects of my daily life', Soofiya admits.

Soofiya's hope is for people to have freedom to be able to govern their own bodies the way they wish and – including removing or keeping any formal body and/or facial hair. Even though we know that hair removal and the way it was advertised in Western society was done in a way to demean women and to make money, we also understand that it is still a choice. The one thing that women lack in most conversations today, on the autonomy of their own bodies, is choice. We find that a lot of the choices are made for us by cis-men. For example, you will see conversations around abortion and many of the people discussing the topic will be cis-men and vitally, many of the people pushing legislation will be cis-men. •

'I think there's value in people drawing bodies that don't look like theirs... particularly in opening up to visibly marginalised bodies.'

**Soofiya**

**S**o when men are removed from the equation, our ideals of beauty rest on us. Maybe then we will find anything and everything beautiful. Meanwhile, internalised misogyny and self-hatred has led to more and more women who find themselves unattractive and not good enough. The problem being the emphasis on beauty, as it's reduction to your outward appearance instead of who you are as a person. And I fell for that.

Of course, my parents would lather me in platitudes of 'you're the most beautiful girl in the world!' and I would return their compliment with a half-arsed smile, wondering if they could see my hesitance. I didn't want my parents to tell me I was beautiful; it was a worthless exercise because they weren't going to fulfil the ultimate goal – to be admired by a man enough to want me. Little did I know how unfulfilling and pointless that act of sex itself was, but as a young, misguided, closeted queer woman, who was easily coerced by media outlets ... I was convinced it was worth it.

And why would a man want to have sex with me, if he wasn't attracted to my face? (Again, this is something I later discovered also didn't matter much.) Despite the hair on the rest of my body, the fascination I had with my facial hair bordered on obsession.

As I got older, I would ask my parents if I could remove my facial hair by going to a beautician like all other girls do for a wax or threading. I was denied of that pleasure (or should I say pain), because I was told my 'hair would only grow back thicker' and I can 'do it when I turn 18'. I wasn't sure what turning 18 did to my hair follicles, but I couldn't take the wait. One day, I sat in my room and threaded my whole face. Tears streamed down my cheek as the thread slipped across my upper lip. I didn't know what to do with my sideburns, so both looked uneven and slanted. I moved onto my neck and in between wiping away tears, managed to remove all hair from my entire face.

I looked at the bright red and in parts bleeding face staring back at me. Strangely, I almost didn't recognise her.

I didn't consider her 'beautiful', just 'different' and to me, different was an improvement. I realised my face was swollen from the threading; my sensitive skin wasn't used to such violence. And so, I sat in front of the mirror for longer, staring at my face, watching the redness subside. It took a couple of hours and I finally felt confident enough to show it off.

But then it hit me. My parents were downstairs, and they would be the first to see it. They would not be happy. I did the direct opposite of what they asked. I wondered how I was going to be able to eat dinner without them realising. Especially since the food goes directly into the area I was intending to hide. I paced my room for a while.

'SHARAN!'

Shit, shit, shit, shit.

'SHARAN!! DINNER!!'

It was now or never. I quietly opened my door, wincing at the creaks it made and how they were especially worse the slower I opened the door. I tiptoed into the landing. Peered over the railing.

All of this by the way was pointless, they were both in the kitchen with the radio on, but I was very aware of my Indian mother's spidey sense, so had to take extra precautions.

I went down the stairs and stood in the living room. The kitchen door was slightly ajar, and I almost wanted them to see me from afar so I didn't have to show them my full face and could run away. I coughed, but the radio was too loud, and mother was on the phone. I crept into the kitchen and stood by the door, as still as a statue, the look on my face of someone who has just committed a horrific murder and didn't hide the body very well.

Dad was the first one who turned and looked at me.

'Sit, food's ready.'

I sat down. He was looking at a newspaper clipping he had cut out, not my face. The tension was killing me. And on cue, mother looked at me.

'What have you done?'

She had hung up the phone and was staring at me.

The Hair Chronicles

# 'My zealously overplucked eyebrows had caused trauma.'

'What happened to your face?'

I ironically felt like I had a hairball stuck in my throat. I couldn't say anything, and I really needed some water but was still re-enacting a statue/murderer, so couldn't move.

My dad had turned to look at me and with confusion, looked back at my mother. He knew something was different but couldn't pinpoint what it was.

'I had to get rid of it all, I hated it, I'm so ugly' and I broke down in tears.

My parents aren't evil, they told me off for disobeying them, but they understood what was happening. A child doesn't break down in front of their parents with a self-inflicted swollen face, without them questioning what caused the behaviour.

My journey from there was one of intense hair removal. I lived through the 90s horror known as the thin eyebrow syndrome and overplucked/threaded them to a millimetre of their lives. What were formerly named 'caterpillars' by bullies became misguided underlines. And they were underlining absolutely nothing. Pointless.

Then I hit my 30s and eyebrows became fashionable. Hair on a woman's face became fashionable. I wasn't as happy about it as you would expect.

My zealously overplucked eyebrows had caused trauma in my follicles and so they would no longer grow back. I was doomed to live with sparse and thin eyebrows.

A young 17-year-old me would never had imagined me writing that. As I glare at women with thick eyebrows, I sat there and drew mine back on. I have gone full circle and I don't like this circle. I remember the kids standing in front of my house calling me ugly, with every hair I draw on. I know that it won't happen with a moustache or chin hair, and eyebrows are a slightly more acceptable form of hair growth, but I couldn't help but feel bitter.

Once again, a woman of colour has had to bear the brunt of the trauma from a facial and body hair positivity revival.

The Hair Chronicles

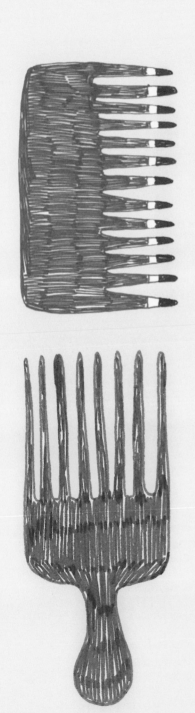

# This blanket of hair is far from comforting

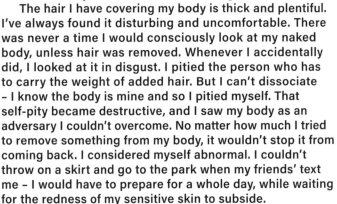

'Gillette for Women. It's a feeling.'

Let me tell you a bit about that feeling.

The hair I have covering my body is thick and plentiful. I've always found it disturbing and uncomfortable. There was never a time I would consciously look at my naked body, unless hair was removed. Whenever I accidentally did, I looked at it in disgust. I pitied the person who has to carry the weight of added hair. But I can't dissociate – I know the body is mine and so I pitied myself. That self-pity became destructive, and I saw my body as an adversary I couldn't overcome. No matter how much I tried to remove something from my body, it wouldn't stop it from coming back. I considered myself abnormal. I couldn't throw on a skirt and go to the park when my friends' text me – I would have to prepare for a whole day, while waiting for the redness of my sensitive skin to subside.

I rejected myself and without realising it, I began to hate myself.

I would cry to my mother, asking why I have so much hair on my body and why hers isn't the same. Why was I afflicted with such an ugly condition? My mother would console me, telling me all people have hair and that I don't have more than everyone. I would reject any consoling. I was busy suffering in self-pity.

I remember dreaming that I would pull out a hair it wouldn't stop, like a clown's handkerchief, it would keep going, and with it, pulling all the excessive hair out of my body and this one long hair, unravelled in front of me was all the hair I didn't want on my body. Gone forever.

Or I would go to a clinic for a hair removal trial, and they would use a laser or cream to permanently and painlessly remove all unwanted hair within seconds. I would walk out free from my hairy shackles.

The thing is, most of these weren't dreams, but half-asleep daydreams, where I would lay in bed, unable to look at my body and attempt to wish away my pain. I would force a fantasy of my future, to bring myself to believe in it enough, that I could live happily. I would lay there and think 'you just have to live like this now but when someone invents a painless hair removal treatment that's cheap and quick, then everything will be fine. Also, they'll invent it very soon. Life will be great.'

'Everything
I did to my
body, was so
I could try and
fit inside a box
that wasn't
designed
for me.'

**S**ome of you may be thinking, that it's just body hair, how and why did I let it affect me the way I did. When I once allowed an ex-boyfriend to see my unshaved legs in a desperate moment for approval, he stated that having sex with me was like sleeping with Ryan Giggs. I know very little about Ryan Giggs, but I can assume he has a fair bit of hair on his legs. I wanted to get so far away from the idea of masculinity as possible, that being considered feminine was the only goal. And being hairless was one of the biggest tick boxes to achieve that. That comment has never left me. I look down at my legs and I think of Ryan Giggs. (Ryan, if you're somehow reading this, it's not your fault.)

The gender binary I was born into created nothing but issues for my mental health – although I am a cis woman, I also know the expected standards of cis women is something I haven't been able to attain to a satisfactory level. I wonder whether that sits me outside of the binary or whether a rejection of beauty standards is the first step in being a fully formed cis woman. I was too young and uninformed to be able to identify any of this and so gender became confusing to me, alongside my sexuality.

It wasn't until I got older that I began to question my sexuality. I surrounded myself with queer people and finally began to understand the concept of gender – in the sense that it was nonsensical. That these standards aren't set by any biological or structural means outside of cis norms that fit into our capitalist society.

And so, removing my body hair was another thing I had to pay society under the table to continue existing there. Because you don't talk about it. Hell no. You're not going to tell anyone your legs look like Ryan Giggs' before you go to the beauticians. Otherwise, those cis men won't sleep with you and society will reject your beauty.

Beauty is intrinsically linked to racism and colourism, although I was unaware of this as a child. Being told to 'clean' my arm or facial hair, was less about hygiene and more about the darkness it reflects on my privileged light skin. God forbid I looked darker due to body hair, and so I was told to remove the excess as soon as I got old enough to be considered for marriage proposals.

My cousins and I would make trips to beauticians'

houses, spread eagle on their makeshift studios at home, while they wax our entire bodies, only to leave hairless, sore and walking like cowboys back to the bus stop. This was a regular occurrence for us. We wouldn't question why we had to do it; we just knew that we should. These aunties would tut at our hair and compliment us when she had finished. 'Look how lovely you look now' they would exclaim as we tear ourselves off the paper sheet stuck onto our butts.

As I got older, I wanted more permanent solutions to the hair on my body and came across the intense pulsed light (IPL) machine – a handheld device that sends a pulse of light onto your skin, to treat melanin in your hair follicles (among other uses). It effectively reduces hair growth, although not removing it completely and permanently. This was my alternative to expensive laser treatments, so I would spend hours attempting to remove hair across my whole face and body, using this nifty device.

I was at a stage where I noticed people talk more about body hair positivity, but I found it to be a very white cis-led movement, with small wisps of blonde hair blowing in the wind from an English rose's armpit. The thick, coarse hair I had did not fit into this movement of positivity and so I continued to remove hair. The IPL device gave me the ability to reduce hair enough, so that when I wanted to be body positive, I could be so in an acceptable way.

I didn't know this when I was younger, but there are a few things that can cause excessive hair growth, such as polycystic ovary syndrome (PCOS), acromegaly or Cushing's syndrome. Most of the causes are to do with an imbalance of hormone levels in your body – high levels of androgen can cause an excess of facial or body hair. PCOS is the most common and goes severely undiagnosed in many people. In 2019, a study published in *The Journal of Obstetrics and Gynaecology Research* showed that increased excess hair was more prevalent in South Asian women with PCOS, when compared with white women.

This is important to note that this is rarely considered when medical checks are done. I remember going to the doctor as a teenager, embarrassed and scared to discuss the hair on my body. As the white doctor looked at my body, frowning, he simply said 'you can just shave', and sent me on my way.

The Hair Chronicles

# Shaving away my shame

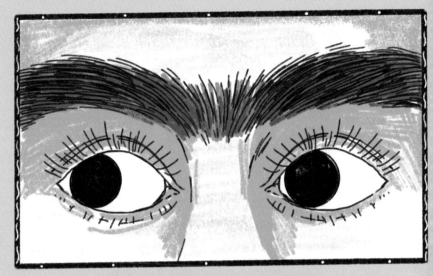

# Interview *with* Marissa Malik

I came across Marissa Malik on
Instagram, when I was promoting
gal-dem's (another amazing
magazine) lockdown event on *Burnt
Roti*. I found an image of her – that
she later told me went viral – of her
pubes and 'snail trail' while holding
a tarot card of The Devil. Marissa
is mixed race Latinx and Pakistani,
so her journey with hair has been
complex. But when discussing body
hair with her, I noticed a distinct
amount of similarities in how we
felt about our bodies.

'The first wave of being able to embrace my body hair, was in my second year of university. I had left the small all-white town I grew up in Connecticut', Marissa tells me, and her accent finally clocks. 'At university, there were a lot of women of colour and non-binary people of colour who were dressed differently and openly queer and sex workers and doing different things with their bodies.'

This was really interesting to me, because despite going to art school myself, I rarely came across this dynamic. In fact, it was a very white university, very cis and in a racist town. I sometimes wonder what my journey would have been like if I was welcomed into a queer, non-cis world at that age. Maybe a lot of it had to do with my own self-hatred and denial of my sexuality. Either way, it fascinates me that others can have this experience.

'The degree I was doing in fine art really encouraged me to interrogate my practice. There was a period of my time in my 20s, during a diaspora politics boom online of embracing culture and heritage, where I basted that in my practice.

I would wax my hair and put it in a book and soak it in beeswax. First it was my legs and I guess that was very represented in the media with body positivity already. But when it came to other areas of my body, especially my stomach trail, which is my money maker, that took time. It actually came from finally embracing that, that I became more confident in my body.'

Marissa laughs when calling her stomach hair her 'money maker', but she knows that existing as herself is seen as radical and at times, marketable. She recognises why this is though.

'I am privileged in that I am relatively thin, and light skinned, and those are compounding factors that make it easier to embrace parts of my body that fat people and people with darker skin can't do as easily.'

I agree wholeheartedly with this. I am seen as conventionally attractive (to some people ... I'm not that full of myself), so if I grow out all of my hair, it would be more acceptable than if it was someone with darker skin or a different body. I'm very aware of that and like Marissa I don't want to victimise myself (I say while writing a whole book about it) because there are reasons

The Hair Chronicles

I am allowed to exist in ways that others aren't.

In many ways I related my body to a man's needs. I truly believed that I needed to look a certain way for someone to like me enough to want to be with me. Can you imagine that? If you're a woman, then yes of course you can. If you're a man, also yes. If you're gender non-conforming or non-binary, this is also true for you. There is no access to beauty that doesn't leave anyone feeling a type of way. Beauty is unattainable for everyone, because it's based on a man's desire, a figment of his imagination.

'A lot of my hair, I used to relate to sexual desire. My mum is Latinx, and would always interrelate hairiness (or lack there of) to how desirable a woman is to a man.' Marissa echoed the same sentiment.

'When I reckoned with my queerness in my early 20s and realised I would be desirable to people regardless of if I had hair or not, I saw it was an option for me. I was really able to embrace my stomach hair when I was in a loving monogamous relationship with someone for three years, where there was space for me to explore different aspects of how I wanted to alter my body without judgement. Being loved by a partner unconditionally, helped me rework that framework in my mind that my mum had created, where I was convinced that no one would desire me by how I looked.'

This is vital, because we need to remember that people will love us for who we are, not for who they want us to be. We aren't hairless beings (I do not want to disregard people with alopecia or other illnesses in this conversation, so I want to say that am referring to the norm, not the reality) so there, in reality, isn't an expectation to be hairless. I guess what we do is believe it to be true, so make it true, despite the pain it causes. Although, the pain that Marissa felt was directly from her family.

'From a really young age I had a monobrow, a really wide one that spread across half my forehead. When I was like 6 or 7, my mum started waxing it, which was really painful and I often had burns on my face because I had really young skin that couldn't handle that. I would cry a lot. Getting my

eyebrows waxed was this horrible violent thing that my mum forced me to do and as a result, I continued the cycle when I was a teenager, to the degree that my eyebrow hair doesn't grow back anymore. I get angry when people ask why I don't have thick eyebrows – it was literally taken away from me, in order for me to societally conform and not be abused by people in my environment.'

I had to stop myself from screaming and interrupting Marissa at this point, because eyebrow hair trauma is something I've discussed already in this chapter. I too over-plucked to an extent that it caused follicle trauma and now, despite the new trend of bushy eyebrows, mine won't return to their normal hairy state. And so

I draw them on. Whiteness allows for eyebrow hair to exist in any form because, quite frankly, everyone has (visible) eyebrow hair. So, it's something they can play with. Whereas stomach hair, butt hair, arm hair etc. isn't always visible – especially with a white/blonde hair type.

Essentially, as Marissa puts it: 'I can't participate in bushy eyebrows and be proud of them because ... racism.'

It's hard to grow up in a way that is considered 'ugly' and people don't forget to let you know.

'Someone pointed out I had hairy nipples once. Often the way I got teased at school was racialised in relation to my hair. It felt like my card that got me in the cult of womanhood, would always be denied as long as that was part of me.' •

R ecently I have started showing my body hair on social media, allowing myself the freedom to exist naturally online. But I know that doing so in real life, in public, where people can laugh and point, will be harder. It may take longer, and the journey will be a ride, but I know that in the end, it will be worth it. Although many people are rude, lacking humanity, for the sake of hiding their own insecurities, causing them to create a commotion about someone else's body ... I also know that it's all very internalised. While many are mean, many just don't care. And some will nod in happy recognition. Mostly, I can throw away that god-awful razor and not have to worry about shaving rash, prickly legs, painful ingrown hairs, traumatising hair removal and importantly, no longer align my worthiness to the ideals of whiteness.

An important acceptance with this is the internalised alignment to sexual experiences and being in queer relationships have helped change my attitude to body hair. It wasn't something I expected, but something I welcomed with open arms. I no longer equated my body hair with my beauty when the women and non-binary people I was with had lived under a similar pressure.

When the women and non-binary people I slept with said 'I couldn't be bothered to shave', I felt a deep love for them, because without them knowing, they were accepting something within me that I had been unable to process. I began to embrace that queer side of me: the side who rejected cis male standards and felt radicalised. I still feel like the hair on my body is excessive and I still remove it at times, but I'm not confined to standards that imprison me. It's a choice I make to grow and unlearn within myself, and the slow process to self-acceptance is ladened with queer love.

Activist and writer Alok V. Menon shared an Instagram post about the book *Plucked: A History of Hair Removal* by Dr. Rebecca Herzig. In the post, they look into the racial history of hair removal, highlighting parts of the texts that discuss the racial intentions behind hair removal.

There is a clear distinction made between animals and people of colour when it came to body hair. Dr. Herzig notes that 'European thinkers argued that hair was a marker of racial difference. New instruments like the trichometer

# 'The slow process to self-acceptance is laden with queer love.'

were designed to quantify hair differences among races. After 1859, many scientists misused Darwin's theory of evolution to argue that race was an evolutionary continuum where 'savages' (racialised people) were closer to animals and white 'civilised' people were the most evolved form of human. In this view, body hair was seen as a marker of animality and degeneracy (an indication that a people had not evolved into civilised humanity).'

It was used as a scientific theory – that people with body hair hadn't evolved like white Europeans and therefore were savages. And this was all policed by white men who controlled the world of advertising, 'As white men became increasingly fixated on controlling white women's beauty regimens, hairlessness became re-signified as a symbol of racial progress and superiority.'

Dr. Herzig quotes historian Peter Stearns, who said that in the 1920s and 1930s 'body hair became disgusting to middle-class American women, it's removal a way to separate oneself from cruder people, lower class and immigrant.' This was done through the marketing of hair removal, the change of fashion and a growing movement of women's independence. The lack of tools for hair removal though, left many with scars and injuries. In an attempt to attain this beauty, people were harming themselves.

The policing of women's bodies has always been within the control of white men, and they have abused that. With the structure in which society exists, men sit at a higher threshold of dominance, through employment and social status and therefore hold the reigns of control. While we continue to defy these standards that men have forced onto us, it's not until power is relinquished that real change can happen. The toppling of systems is where is starts, from Parliament to policing – this is where men have the ability to govern us without reprimand. •

# 3

# MY BODY IS A TEMPLE

The hook in my nose

**D**on't sneeze for a week!
I repeat the words in my head while staring at the wry smile on my surgeon's face as he waves goodbye. It's the day I'm discharged from Harley Medical Clinic after my nose job and I wonder whether it's the drugs that are making his smile seem insidious, or the blurriness of my sore and puffy eyes. Maybe it's the drugs. I furrow my brow. Or I think I've furrowed my brow; my face is numb. I'm bound to sneeze. What would happen? Would it explode? It's all I can think about.

It was a week later when I returned to the clinic that I realised I hadn't actually sneezed. I wait politely for the nurse to stop asking me crucial health related questions before I let her now.

'I didn't sneeze', I say smugly as she fiddled with my plasters.

'Okay.'

I am far too attention-seeking and anxious for that indifferent response.

'I mean, I was told not to sneeze, which I thought was weird, because you can't really control that can you?', I continue rambling,

'Especially since I have hay fever, so sneezing is essentially part of my personality.'

She's bemused, and I'm not sure whether it's because no one's ever been told not to sneeze, or simply because it's all I'm talking about.

'You're barely bruised, which is great. We're going to take the stitches out now and you're good to go.' In hindsight, I appreciate her ability to weave around my awkward announcements.

In the car home, I take selfies of my swollen yet smaller nose. I couldn't stop looking at myself in the car mirror. I knew I was going to look different, but there was nothing

'There were only two types of attention I was going to get at school: negative or none.'

I could compare myself to. I had to wait for the swelling to go down to really see the difference, but alas, I didn't give myself that chance.

That night I went out and broke my nose.

Let me come back to that night in a moment. Here's where I build the tension.

I hated school, and it wasn't because I didn't want to learn anything, in fact I loved a select few subjects and really enjoyed socialising with the two (or was it three?) friends I had.

School was just another place I felt vulnerable and exposed – and it was particularly difficult because people can really be little shits. There were only two types of attention I was going to get at school: negative or none.

Let's not put all the blame on young people, though – the first time I really became aware of my nose, an aunty had made a joke about its size. Her head tilted back as she poured the crumbs of a ladoo into her mouth, wiping her hands and smiling – all while staring directly at me. It didn't feel funny. Not just because it was harmful to say, but because her eyes weren't laughing. While she stared at me – while she made the room laugh at the expense of a young child's appearance – her eyes burned disappointment into me. 'Why can't you be prettier?' they said. 'Why can't you make it easier for us to marry you off?'

I was eight years old when I realised I was ugly.

That pain transmitted out of me without my control, and I draped my insecurities all over myself, like a sharp and wet blanket. People took notice. Bullies took notice. I used to love Disney's Pinocchio until one day I just couldn't watch it anymore. That word no longer conjured magical visuals of a young puppet inside a whale, but instead of kids interrupting class when I answered a question with 'she's lying! You can tell from her nose!!'

At university, a boyfriend at the time (and let me use the term boyfriend loosely, because he was an absolute mug), during a moment of silence as we were watching Extreme Makeover: Home Edition (a staple in our house), turned to me and said 'would you ever get a nose job?'

I didn't know how to react. I told him I would consider it, but for me not for anyone else. He seemed satisfied. But I'm not. I still think of it to this day. Did anyone else think that but never say it? How many people wished they could change my face?

My mother once said to me that the little wart-like bump on my nose was irritating and when we went to the doctor to burn it off, she said 'good, now you can find someone' and I realise it comes from a place of innocence, but it's riddled me with issues. I related my looks to my value and wondered why my mental health was compromised. There was nothing 'wrong' with my nose and I don't regret getting it done. The nose job saved me in many ways. It's a sad thing to say; that my beauty mattered to me so much. But it still does. I still worry if a photo is posted of me that doesn't shine me in the perfect light. I used to photoshop the wart-like bump off my nose in photos before posting anything – 'No one would want me with it'. I believed what my mother had said.

'I related my looks to my value and wondered why my mental health was compromised.'

# Dealing with bullying

Sometimes it can feel impossible
to think of it this way, but a lot of the
time, there's a reason why someone
treats you badly and usually it's
something personal to them. A lot
of people have insecurities, and these
can come out in different ways. Some
project onto others around them.

This isn't helpful at the time though,
it's just interesting knowledge to have.
I found a group of people who
were similarly bullied and formed
friendships within them. It created
a sense of solidarity. When I isolated
myself, the loneliness was a big
instigator of sadness.

I didn't do well in school because
of this, but I wish I did channel
that energy into something more
productive other than criticising

myself. I was always interested
in art and graphic design but wouldn't
put any effort in my work. I was curious
and my sexuality was confusing me
at that time. It wasn't easy to be seen
as ugly, all while dealing with puberty.
When looking back, I recognise
the amount of people dealing with
the same issues – whether it was
interrogating their own sexuality
or the concept of sex itself. Again,
isolating myself as a singular victim
meant I couldn't see the bigger picture.

When I did turn to my parents,
I found their support was the backbone
I needed to finish school. I know now
I wasn't on the bullies' minds as much
as they were on mine, and my parents
helped me conquer that. Eventually,
art and music saved me. Comic books,
David Lynch and Bollywood.
A focus came to me and I was able
to create something from it.

did not plan on breaking my nose the day I had my stitches removed. In fact, I was consumed with the need to protect it. I feared people in my vicinity, in case they carelessly bumped into me, pressing on my nose and bursting it open.

Yet, when my cousin text me saying we should celebrate my new nose with drinks at Yates, in Hounslow, I was too enamoured with alcohol as a 20-something to decline. It wasn't just that I hadn't drank in a couple of weeks or seen anyone other than my parents or doctors, I wanted to show off my new – swollen but new – nose. My outrageous disregard for my own anxiety – the one thing I know I can count on, turned into my nightmare.

There was myself, my cousin, a friend of mine 'A' and around four other people I had never seen before, all congregating at the worst bar imaginable, to celebrate my new nose. We were transfixed – guided in by cheap strobe lighting bursting through the nailed-shut windows with sweaty men pressed up against them – imagine a siren song, but the siren can't sing.

We were broke, yet young. Ready to take on the night, while clutching a £10 note in our pockets and hoping the overt sexual desires of men would enable our drinking. While ordering a drink, I'm stuck between two men and accidentally place my arms on a wet bar. Grimacing I move to wipe my arms and accidentally bump my nose.

'FOR FUCK'S SAKE'

Everyone looks at me as I hurriedly check my nose for blood. There's nothing there, it's just sore and honestly … I barely even stroked it. The faces glaring at me in apathy have turned away again and like a film, the music and chatter seems to get louder. No one's bought me a drink. I return to the table, hunched over in defeat, with a watered-down rum and coke in my hand. Luckily everyone at my table's distracted so don't notice my disdain, but unluckily for me, it was because a fight had broken out next to us. A group of what seemed like Indian boys (diamond earring, speaking with Black vernacular and driving their dad's souped-up cars) were arguing with a group of Polish men about what I some may call 'cultural nuance', but in reality, they were being a bunch of dicks. I'm pretty sure I heard an Indian guy yell 'go back to your country' and I stare at him bemused. While I contemplate this contradiction, I don't notice my friend A hop to the middle of the group enquiring loudly 'what's happening here?'

'Fuck.'

I jump up to grab her but we're in the firing range and I as she turns to look at me with the sweetest smile on her little face, a man elbows me directly on my new nose. A's grabbed and punched in the face. We're both on the floor and my t-shirts covered in blood and tears. A bouncer picks us up, by what feels like the scruff of our necks and swiftly throws us behind the bar, shoving tissues on our face before announcing 'I'll be back.' I still picture Arnold Schwarzenegger when I think of him. He goes back to break up the fight and we're left to fend for ourselves.

In the taxi on the way back, I pray my parents are still asleep; my dad spent £5,000 on my new nose from his savings and I can't let him know that the day I got my stitches removed, I broke my nose again. I fly in through the door and up the stairs, closing my door quietly like an expert and quickly remove my t-shirt. I wrap a shirt around me (I refuse to pull anything over my head ever again) and head to the bathroom, where I clean my face.

'They'll never know' I tell myself.

Mum, dad – if you're reading this, I'm sorry. One nostril is slightly closed, and the bridge is broken again. I was told it wasn't my fault – I can't control the aggressive elbows of cruel racist men, but I could have held back from going out. I mean, especially Yates, in Hounslow. I might as well have headbutted a wall as soon as I came out of surgery.

I went downstairs the next day and my nose was freshly swollen.

'Oooh, it looks more swollen!' my mum exclaims, and I manage to convince her that it's how swelling works and suddenly I've successfully re-written science. I was ridden with guilt. I couldn't tell them that I broke it, especially since I did it while drinking.

My parents understood my struggles with my nose and had accepted this journey for me, with no judgement. I understand now that it's a complex situation. Not only was I suffering with mental health issues, body disorders and bullying, I was nearing an age to get married and they probably wanted me to look my best. I think about that often and consider what looking my 'best' means. Was my Indian nose not good enough? Was my Indian-ness not good enough?

# Interview *with*
# Robyn Wilder

The first time I considered how my ethnicity was tied to my nose was when journalist Robyn Wilder wrote an article for *Cosmopolitan* titled 'I Have A Very "Ethnic" Nose'.

Investigating how cosmetic enhancements intersect with different ethnic community values was an idea Robyn had been pitching to mainstream magazines for years. 'Mostly without success', she told me. 'Publications were interested until they realised I wasn't offering some lurid exposé about people achieving whiteness through surgery, largely because it doesn't exist.

'My interest was specifically in the "ethnic-ness" of the cosmetic enhancements themselves; how specialist cosmetic surgeons make cosmetic changes while actively preserving patents' cultural identity.

'I'm fascinated by what that must entail. Are there guidelines, gradations of "ethnicity" features? How subjective is it? How do

you measure the cultural qualities of a *nose*?'

Shockingly (this is sarcasm), publishing platforms are saturated with whiteness, so don't believe there is value in these stories. They don't believe the readership exists. Well, they especially didn't in 2016. If *Burnt Roti* has shown anything, it's that there is a thirst for these stories.

Robyn is frequently a go-to name for 'brownness' stories in the media – but she does turn work down.

'Although I work the "brown beat", sometimes I have to explain I'm just not brown enough to cover certain angles or topics with authority. I wouldn't want to be a false mascot for a community I'm not involved in, or know nothing about.

'It's not publishing's fault that some people see me as a brown lady, and as such briefed by the brown PR people on the latest brown-approved news comment. Since my early teens, everyone, from best friends to doctors to random racists in the street, has seen me as a *"de facto"* Asian.

'But I'm Italian and Spanish on my father's side, and French and Nepali on my mother's. My Asianness is so diluted that, if I was white-skinned, I'd still count as white. But often when I first meet people they're

surprised I even speak English at all. Presumably because my skin is brown. I am that rarest of things, ethnically three-quarters Western European, but *brown-passing*.'

This brings in an important conversation around mixed race people and the racism they face. I have spoken to 'white passing' friends who have experienced unpleasant situations where white people have felt comfortable making racially charged comments.

There seems to be little benefit to being 'brown-passing' either. As a teenager Robyn experienced racism at school, sometimes violent – just as I did – but her ethnicity was perceived.

'I went to school with a bunch of skinny, hairless, buttoned-nosed blonde girls, was bullied viciously on a daily basis for my "hairy shit

My Body Is A Temple

curry" looks, and didn't have anyone to confide in. The UK Latina-Franco-Nepali community stands at one, and there was a language barrier with the other Asian girls (I couldn't speak Hindi or Urdu because I wasn't that sort of Asian).

'Some nights I'd to bed praying to wake up blonde. In the end it didn't really matter how Asian I was or wasn't. Ultimately, it was my mixedness that kept me afloat until I could leave school and see it all in perspective. As a child I was lucky enough to live in Argentina and the USA, where I'm just Latina; and in Italy where I'm *un po 'più in là* ("Italian and a little bit extra").'

I think a lot about the genes we pass onto our children – what features or aspects from us will they get? Will they get my (old) nose? My hairiness? Would they have to go through the same trauma I did?

'I'm now a mother myself, and I've added my English-German husband's DNA to my own, to produce two boys – one blond, one brunette, both white. So white, in fact, that I'm frequently mistaken for their nanny, or – at least once – that I have stolen them. I guess the reason I'm so fascinated by

how people measure racial physical characteristics is because I don't really believe such things objectively exist. Exposure to, and enthusiastic celebration of all my cultures laid a good foundation for me, I want to do the same for my sons.

'They will grow up white boys, in a white country, but hopefully ones who appreciate their own slightly hidden cultural mix. If I'm a fake Asian, perhaps my kids are Stealth Ethnics, and can start challenging the system from the inside.'

I think that's where we have to stew for a while, because while I talk about whiteness being the absolute, there is an inability to escape my inherent brownness. When I change my nose, hairiness, if I even changed my skin colour – my children will have it all. It's still inside me and nothing on the outside can change that.

I find that beautiful. Not feeling the need to obtain to whiteness, of course – but knowing that even when these pressures get to us – we are still there, deep down.

If my children, through the trials and errors of IVF, donors, eggs etc, don't have a lot of my features, they will be living with and experiencing my life. •

My Body Is A Temple

'I went
to school with
a bunch of
skinny, hairless,
buttoned-nosed
blonde girls.'

**Robyn Wilder**

There is a history of people seeking white-centric features through plastic surgery and one of the most famous cases discussed is Michael Jackson. In an interview with Oprah Winfrey, he admits to rhinoplasty, although saying he never consciously tried to remove his Blackness. He talks about being proud of being Black. Oprah asks if he ever looks in the mirror and thinks 'I look pretty cute today' and he nervously laughs before saying he's never happy and tries not to look in the mirror.

He goes on to make a point to say 'If everyone in Hollywood who has had plastic surgery was told to go on holiday, the place will be empty.'

That rings true – surgery isn't uncommon, it is in fact an expectation for celebrities. Celebrities that fall into ideal white beauty standards usually have minimal surgery, whereas those that don't can sometimes go to an extreme to reach these standards.

Other than Michael Jackson, one of the most discussed celebrities, when it comes to ethnic cleansing through surgery, is probably Lil' Kim. And while I can sit here and list a name of celebrities who have undergone surgery to achieve a white-centric beauty standard, I'm not here to 'out' people. I want to demonstrate how prevalent it is in our society, usually pushed onto us from the beauty industry, which is governed by celebrity culture.

Lil' Kim has undergone a lot of surgery, where people questioned her intentions to remove her Blackness – through skin lightening and reduction of the size of her nose. While some people were critical of her, many found themselves questioning the pressures she's under. As a Black woman in a male dominated industry, dubbed as the

'Queen of Rap', her sex-positive lyrics laid the path for Black female rappers to take hold of their sexuality in their music. We don't all have the pressures faced by people like Lil' Kim, but we can't disregard the ongoing oppression of a person's anatomy over their own body.

Journalist Rachael Krishna filmed a piece for *Buzzfeed* where she went to South Korea for a consultation on surgery on her face. It highlights how South Korea has one of the highest rates of plastic surgery in the world, a lot of which comes from international tourists. A 2011 report from the International Society of Aesthetic Plastic Surgery suggested that most of their procedures are eyelid and jaw surgeries.

I wonder whether that bank of information would have been useful for me. I don't think I would have done anything differently. My nose job meant I wouldn't have anxiety every time someone looked at my profile or people made jokes about Concordes or how I would accidentally 'slap someone across the face by merely turning my head'. I was able to exist as myself and not have to worry about being known as 'the girl with that nose'. But that's my experience and frankly, I was susceptible to these comments because my thick glasses and moustache allowed for it. I was already a target for bullies and so I dug deeper into a hole of despair.

'If everyone in Hollywood who has had plastic surgery was told to go on holiday, the place will be empty.'

(Michael Jackson)

# Nose Affirmations

I know!
Yours is so
weird and small
though ...

Every shape of me
is passed down from
an ancestral lineage
of beautiful women.

Keep your
nose out of my
business.

Thanks!
You have
lovely eyes.

Everything about me is
desirable. From the curve
of my chest. The curve
of my hips. The curve
of my nose.

Are you...
Are you
hitting
on me ...?

speak to people now about my nose and when they tell me about their apprehensions about their appearance, I always say 'I understand'. There's nothing wrong with someone questioning their looks – we live in a world that tells us to care. My culture tells me to look my best so I can get married, the media tells me perfection can only be reached by whiteness and jobs tell me to 'look presentable' – I always read that as 'pretty and thin'. If I had a moustache, would that 'front of desk' job have hired me? If I hadn't spent an hour meticulously plucking every hair off my face in the morning, would they have sent me home?

I still focus on my nose, aware of the second time I broke it. 'We can't tell!' my friends say, but I can. It's slightly askew and sometimes I think I can feel it move. I went on BBC News Facebook live years later to talk about my surgery and the comments under the post was littered with racism and sexism – some commenting on my other features but those that said, 'so when is she getting the nose job?' hit me hard. This nose cost £5k, it was done by an expert surgeon. Did I need another one? I considered it; I'm not going to lie. For a short while, I wondered if I should contact my surgeon and tell him I broke it again, asking if he could fix it. I would daydream going to his office and out of sympathy, he would perform it right away, putting a small plaster on it and sending me on my way as I skip back home. I fall on my face and break it again in my daydream, by the way.

I stand at a very awkward stage with it now, where I realise that the values I had about who I was supposed to be led me to have plastic surgery. Despite that, I don't regret my choice to have a nose job. I understand that it isn't fair that the little time we have here, should be consumed with thoughts of inadequacy. It isn't fair that women and especially women of colour should have to deal with this additional pressure for merely existing.

But getting a nose job to gain confidence did not (unfortunately) rid my life of the patriarchy. The systems we live with led me to believe there was more that I needed to change.

My nose was the centre of this – it was the focus, almost like the vanishing point in a one-point perspective drawing. I believed that when I 'fixed' it, everything would resolve itself. Little did I realise that my new focus would be replaced with everything else about me that was considered 'unattractive'.

My Body Is A Temple

# My body curves into a spiral

**\* TRIGGER WARNING:
EATING AND BODY DISORDERS \***

I was always thin growing up – my legs looked like twigs and people would make jokes about 'snapping them in half', which I honestly don't think adults should say to a child, even as a joke. As a large man cowers over me, to make this comment, his eyes large and lips curved in a horrific smile, I shudder. I think of his large hands grabbing me and snapping me. I think of how easy it is. That was the first time I noticed my body. I was 6.

My mother was adamant I would be a healthy child, and so I was entered into every sport in the Southall area. I joined clubs, played tennis, badminton, gymnastics, trampolining, kung fu, judo ... the list goes on. I was on a schedule of school, homework and sport and it was to keep my body in line. It was a way of regulating my appearance – without me realising, I was being moulded.

While I kept to this schedule as a child, it was in my teens that I started to reject the regimented life and stopped going to most sports clubs, instead frequenting the local KFC and discovering alcohol. Despite having hair all over my body and face, a nose I wasn't happy with, bad eyesight, a crooked smile and diminishing self-esteem, I believed my body was my saving grace. I would say 'at least my body looks good', and I would say that in comparison to celebrities. My breasts were small and my hips weak, but I was thin like them.

Stopping all exercise meant that I was allowing my body to change naturally with my somewhat reckless decisions – but it was my decision. Although it has affected me negatively in the long run – after years of exercise, a sudden stop meant my already slightly deformed bones started to hurt more. When I say slightly deformed, I mean my hip is imbalanced (my physio once told me that if my pelvis was a bowl of water, I'd be constantly spilling liquid), my knees and my ankles turn in and my back is ... well, my back is a mess.

I can't really remember how I learnt I had eating disorders but when my friend once looked at me after not seeing me for a few months, saying 'Sharan ... have you been eating?'

I realise I hadn't.

'Mum just makes loads of vegetarian food and I hate it, so I don't eat much at home', I replied laughing. In reality, that was a terrible excuse and my mum would make loads of meat-based food, but I didn't want to eat because I wanted to look sexy. And so I would go a day without eating and then have one meal the next day. But that meal would make me feel heavy and large and so I would have a laxative to try and flush it out of me.

This happened with no one noticing. I had moved back home after university and after a misstep (to put it nicely) with an ex (the same one who had asked me if I wanted to get a nose job mid an *Extreme Makeover* binge), I was working an office job in Hounslow. I was barely at the house and when I was, my family was out. We weren't avoiding each other; we were just living our lives.

I would go to the pub a lot to make up for eating. I would drink until I was sick. And a lot of the time it was on an empty stomach, harming myself further. While I acknowledged that what I was doing probably wasn't healthy, I never considered it a disease. I was just 'doing this for a bit until I was happy with my body' and the time I thought I was going to spend doing it lasted years.

My mental health began to improve through various changes in my lifestyle. I found moving away from home helped – not away from my family in particular, but from a familiarity of trauma I had felt in that area. I began to find new ways to console my addiction to beauty. Although my relationship with food has always been confusing – I either enjoyed it enough to eat in a healthy manner, or I avoided it completely – my new fascination was with taking selfies and photoshopping them. I lived digitally because my real self wasn't good enough.

My Body Is A Temple

# Interview *with* Alia

*Name changed for anonymity

It was important for me to have this discussion with someone else, because disordered eating can feel really insular and without a connection or validity, there's fear in becoming trapped in self-doubt.

I was interested in how eating disorders and our culture plays a part outside of the expectations of marriage. Alia revealed how being Muslim and dealing with Ramadan was a big part of her life when coping with her food intake.

'The first time I remember having any disordered eating, I was about 16 or 17 and I was experiencing depression, although I hadn't identified it as that yet. I had low self-esteem ever since 12 or 13, made worse with experiences of bullying and being made to feel unattractive and unwanted. It was when I was 17 I can quite clearly remember that one of my friends telling me she was worried about me, because she had asked me what I had for lunch one day and I said I had a plate of carrot and celery and hummus and that was it. I didn't think anything of it – I considered it healthy and an attempt to lose weight – those two things were synonymous to me at the time.'

Alia's experience at university is where it really took its toll on her. She was a high-achiever, but when attending Cambridge University, where everyone was a high-achiever, she lost any sense of identity that she could control.

'It was very clear I stuck out like a sore thumb, I was Asian (in a predominately white institution) and I didn't drink (there's a strong drinking culture there), so I felt like I stuck out. And now I wasn't the smart one in the room, and I didn't know how to define myself anymore. I didn't want to be the brown one who didn't drink. A decision I didn't consciously make was to be the small one – the skinny one. This gave me a goal I could work towards.'

In her second year, she explains that it got its worst when she came back from summer break to start the year and stopped looking for support from professionals.

'I remember one day; I only ate a banana the whole day and was smoking with friends and I nearly passed out because I was super lightheaded and my friend had to feed me. I went back to the GP asked them if they could give me supplements and they said: 'no you just have to eat'. But they gave me anti-depressants that I was taking on an empty stomach. Two days into them I felt like my stomach was going to come out of my body because I was in so much pain. At that point I had to call my family and tell them I was in pain. My brother drove up and had a frank discussion about what was going on. I think letting that happen, having that conversation, made a huge change.'

Disordered eating is something that stays with you in life for many people and it's about how you manage it. Whether it's through lifestyle changes, therapy and medical assistance, you have to find ways to maintain the desires to harm yourself. It's especially difficult for Alia as a Muslim woman.

'Ramadan gave me an excuse not to eat. From 17 onwards, it was an effective cover under which not to eat. It was accepted as an excuse – I was fasting, so I wasn't meant to. It was a good cover for that.'

But as someone who is recovering, it adds more elements of uncomfortable experiences.

'I can't fast because of my eating disorder, and it would be quite a risk to my mental and physical health. The hardest part is people feel they have the right to ask you why you aren't fasting. They feel like you're obligated to report to them. There are lots of different medical reasons why someone can't fast, like I have friends and family members who suffer from migraines, so they can't go the whole day without food or water – it's a risk to their health. Also, if you're on medication and you need to take it on specific times in the day, you have to take it with water and food. When you're on your period, you can't fast and I don't want to have to tell people I'm on my period.'

Alia reminisces about taking part in Ramadan in the same way other Muslims do. She feels a sadness from not being able to because of her health, but also understands the importance of not taking part.

'I miss fasting because there's a community spirit during Ramadan in my community and communities around the world. A big part of being able to feel the spirit is by taking part in the month of fasting. I've been looking for other ways to observe it, such as donating to charity because that's a big aspect to Ramadan. Or trying to look after my friends and family who are fasting by making them food they like or specific treats.'

It's tricky. Alia mentions how it's Muslims and non-Muslims who ask her these uncomfortable questions that she has to respond to, in order to prove her commitment to Islam. But there are ways to support people during these moments.

'The important thing is being upfront with the people who are close to me. I remember I went to a Iftar a few years ago, none of us were fasting for health reasons, and we had it anyway and it was nice, because it felt like we were still observing Ramadan.'

'Mental health in general isn't discussed in many communities, such as in Muslim and South Asian communities, and that has made it difficult to explain why I'm not fasting. But it's also made it more difficult to come to terms with it because I didn't have the language to talk about it and didn't know how I would explain it to people in my life. Most people have been sympathetic and understanding but most of my extended family know about it and my immediate family aren't sure about what it all means, but they have been really supportive.'

I think this is important. When people suffer from mental health issues and disordered eating, there isn't a space to discuss it in many South Asian communities. Sometimes that leaves the person who suffers feeling isolated and spiral further. Sometimes it makes them doubt the seriousness of their health and continue to enact harm. •

As it has only recently been recorded that eating disorders within South Asian women was prevalent – in fact in many Black, Asian and minority ethnic communities – and I wonder whether it's for a similar reason. Whether attaining a certain beauty standard outside of our reach was the focus.

In a 2018 study, '"I'm not White, I have to be pretty and skinny": A qualitative exploration of body image and eating disorders among Asian American women', found that 'Across several studies, Asian American women maintain levels of body dissatisfaction at rates equal to or higher than representative samples of other racial and ethnic groups (Frederick, Forbes, Grigorian, & Jarcho, 2007; Frederick, Kelly, Latner, Sandhu, & Tsong, 2016; Stark-Wroblewski, Yanico, & Lupe, 2005) ... in a meta-analysis conducted across U.S. and non-U.S. samples by Wildes, Emery, and Simons (2001), women of Asian ancestry exhibited higher levels of eating pathology for behaviours such as weight and dieting concerns, dietary restraint, body dissatisfaction, smaller ideal body, and lower reported weight than White women.'

It feels like there is a pattern here and studies weren't conducted on this until recently. It can come down to a few things, as pointed out in the study, '(1) Societal influence of mainstream White culture and Asian culture; (2) interpersonal influences of immediate family and close others; and (3) individual influence.'

The first point '(1) Societal influence of mainstream White culture and Asian culture' is the enforcement of the importance of beauty on women. Whichever culture you are in, a woman will be defined by her beauty and there's no escaping that. The second point '(2) interpersonal influences of immediate family and close others', to me, refers to the pressures from family to look good enough to be married. And we're back to that conversation – Asian women and in my experience, Indian women exist to please men in servitude and sexually. The final point '(3) individual influence' adds the nuance of saying not everyone's focus around their beauty defines them as strongly as others, which could eventually lead to body disorders. While I focused heavily on how I was perceived by others, I was aware that women around me weren't as worried about it. Well, at least not vocally.

As I've gotten older and made changes to my appearance, whether it's through surgery, hair removal or the trauma of eating disorders, I now fit neatly into a beauty ideal that's acceptable. People find me attractive and tell me that. But with this comes self-doubt and a need to maintain this appearance of beauty I've somehow upheld – through posed photos online, to perfectly applying make up prior to social events.

Triggers can come at any time and sometimes, they are not so obvious. For example, if I experience rejection in certain a romantic situation, I resort back to causing myself harm. I guess it doesn't start off well, because I feel that once I have fooled someone into thinking I am worthy to be with, I worry they will realise I am not. Relationships don't always work out, I'm not saying every time someone says they don't want to be with me, I stop eating. But when I've been hurt maliciously, in comparison to whiteness (being left for a white person), I blame myself. And so I work again on being attractive enough for someone to want to stay. My initial negative thoughts on my beauty become reality and I realise that I will never fit into the perfect box. When I'm cheated on for a white person, I look at my brown skin and wonder why it isn't good enough. I wonder if my nipples are too brown, |my pussy too dark, my body hair too coarse, my eyes not bright enough, my culture too obtrusive, my activism too … guilt inducing.

The thing is … this is common. I've had far too many conversations with women of colour having to deal with their partners rejecting or cheating on them with a white girl. A Becky, in fact. (The name Becky was made popular from Beyonce's song 'Sorry', when referencing a 'basic' woman). And this Becky doesn't just ruin a relationship, they trigger a suffocating self-hatred. This Becky isn't the individual person, but the concept of whiteness.

After a while and through the process of healing, it becomes clearer that despite white privilege playing a heavy part in causing harm, it isn't us who do it. It is easy to compare yourself to white people and yearn to find beauty in the most basic of appearances (rosy cheeks, light eyes etc.), when women of colour have to try so hard to be accepted, but it's that moment of clarity where we remember how desirable we are, despite this.

'My coarse hair is reminiscent of the heavy locks on my head that white people desire. My culture is something white people try to emulate with appropriation ... my food will always taste better. My eyes are filled with the art and history of my ancestors. My tongue can speak the languages you can't decipher.'

With accepting our individuality, comes our beauty. When you view the simplicity of whiteness as 'easy', you realise that you're not a problem, it's just harder for a white person to align themselves to your complexity. Many of them have lived their lives without having to face, understand or acknowledge the complexity of racial issues, so when they are with a non-white person, a lot of the time, they're not ready for the realities of the world. This isn't an 'all white people can't be with PoC' statement, it's a 'this is why it's complicated' statement.

Some people may consider this resentment from previous experiences, which is fine. Maybe it is! I'm not someone who truly means it when she claims to know it all, I just say it for attention. Someone once tweeted me when I said something about being fucked over by a white person with something along the lines of: 'Maybe stop dating white people then???' and I laughed. Mostly because they called me out without holding back. While my dating history isn't all white, the most recent people are. But I find issue in this response.

The person I have loved more than anything in the world is a white woman. Does that cause direct harm? Maybe. But it's a personal harm I have chosen. Whether I continue to allow that harm is something I will decide on my own. And I will talk about the complications and I will vent. We need to allow for compassion and access here. I have previously fallen in love with a white woman, sure. Doesn't mean I can't call out all the problems that came alongside it.

I'm going to be poetic here, hold onto your seats. My ability to love isn't the same as my ability to hate. I hate white systems; I have loved white people. I hate the pain whiteness has and continues to inflict, I love the intimacy a white person has previously given me. You may see them as contradictions, and that's cool, because in many ways they are. The point I'm making is the ability to love and the ability to hate are two different things, they come from two different places inside you. But I will put more of my energy in fighting the systems that cause white supremacy than I will the people that inhabit it. And with that, I allow space for love. Anyway, we all know I'm going to end up alone, in some boujee apartment, with far too many animals, which are evidently only there to replace the affection a person can give. If only you can see the smile that sentence created. In many ways, it's an ideal.

Alas, despite any revelations, with rejection comes depression and with depression comes shame. Eating disorders have been a big part of my life, but it's only when an unprecedented spanner is thrown in the works do they really shine.

'Hi!! Eating shame here!!! I'm back! Now lay down, don't move and definitely don't eat. Maybe this bed can swallow you up.'

The road to recovery is long and hard but absolutely important. It doesn't come with just eating, it comes with the way I view myself. If I start trying to eat a lot, I will hate myself, causing myself to dislike my body more. But if I change the conversation I have with myself from 'you're not worthy' to 'you're actually alright', then I have a chance to recover. Looking at my naked body and celebrating my ageing face has led to a positive amount of eating and exercise. That switch isn't easy to do but it is possible. I have done it a number of times. And I'm super lazy.

# I still can't see clearly now

The things I went through to fit into a beauty standard that wasn't built for me, my dear god. Let me tell you. Wearing glasses was the icing on the Groucho Marx cake and I had really bad eyesight, so they were those thick glasses, where the lenses were three times the thickness of the frame.

I was ready to be glasses-free. I switched to contact lenses, but regularly fell asleep in them, overused them and got various eye infections off the back of it. It was time to let go of this responsibility that I clearly couldn't handle. There was a phenomenon happening at the time, with many South Asian women, of wearing coloured contact lenses – and I joined this craze with 'hazel' and 'grey' colours. My dark brown eyes were no longer shielded behind glasses, but I wanted them to be lighter, like that of white people. Their eyes were beautiful and reflected the light in a stunning way. I had convinced myself lighter eyes were ideal, so regularly wore lenses that were not my natural dark brown eye colour.

Just like one of the most famous photos ever taken, of the Afghan girl with green eyes by white voyeur Steve McCurry, I wanted to be coveted. I'm not sure what changed in me, maybe it was because those contact lenses were so terribly made that my eyes looked alien-like or because literally every Asian woman I knew also suddenly had green eyes – I stopped wearing them. But I still wanted to rid myself of the chore of poking my eyeballs every time I went to bed.

So, I asked to get laser eye surgery. My parents had considered it for themselves but thought their kids would benefit from it greater – my brother's eyesight was as bad, if not worse than mine, so we both decided we were getting it done.

After going to a consultation at Specsavers and realising the procedure would cost around £4,000, my parents switched on their Indian money-saving skills and contacted family in Punjab. Within a week, we had found an accredited surgeon who would perform the surgery for a tenth of the original price, booked flights to India (mother works for

'I had convinced myself lighter eyes were ideal, so regularly wore lenses that were not my natural dark brown eye colour.'

British Airways, so that was relatively simple), and told aunties and uncles we were staying with them. The amount we saved was spoken about for years after. The pride! 'Look at how much these British people are paying for this, the idiots!' It was on the flight to India that I considered my privilege. If I didn't have parents who allowed me to change my appearance, who could get a flight, who had saved enough for my nose job, I wouldn't be where I am today. Albeit questioning my very existence, I live relatively comfortably knowing I've made these changes.

I want to make this clear – I live with trauma and health issues (physical and mental), but I am not the spokesperson on attractiveness because I live with privilege. Light skin and thin privilege being the major ones and to be honest, the most prevalent in society. This is a collection of stories of my experiences and noticed behaviours, not a call for people to 'look how ugly I am', because it's not.

When we get to Punjab, we stay with our family, and it feels relaxed. We go to markets, eat too much food, sit on the manjai outside or on the roof, drink cha and talk about people I've never met. Then the day comes for the consultation with our surgeon and I'm so relaxed at this point, you can pour me into a beautifully adorned colonial tea set.

We walk into the reception area and it's teaming with people. We manage to find someone standing around the reception desk, they take our names, and we join the queue of patients waiting outside the doctor's office. As I sit there, I start to become anxious. I realise I'm bound to have surgery in a day or two and it could go horribly wrong, and I'll be left blinded and scarred. I try to push these thoughts away, but it's surgery – it shouldn't be taken lightly. As we wait, a person occasionally approaches us and pours eyedrops into our eyes in preparation for seeing the doctor. We're there for about an hour until we're called in and I go first.

There are two types of surgery we could have (skip this part of you're squeamish) – either they slice the cornea, lift it and shoot a laser into your eye that way. It works if your cornea is thick enough to slice and return to heal. The other option, if your cornea is too thin, is to just shoot a laser straight into your goddamn eye like a badass.

Luckily, I didn't have to be a badass, and so they opted for slicing my cornea. I didn't realise at the time I was lucky, because my brother had to have direct laser treatment because of his thin ass cornea and his healing period was weeks long.

I mention the eyedrops we were given while waiting.

'What eyedrops', the doctor asks while filling out paperwork.

'You know, your receptionists were putting stuff in our eyes', I say trying to get eye contact. The anxiety was coming back.

He looks up at us and laughs 'My receptionist is off today, those are her friends, they like to just hang around here'.

The anxiety has come on full force now and I glare at my mum.

'What were they putting in my eyes???' I'm burning a hole into him with my eyes, trying to create my own lasers.

'Oh they only have saline solution at reception, it's nothing, harmless, don't worry ... so, tomorrow we will pick you up ...'

He trails off and my mum is looking at my panicked face while trying to take in the information he's giving us. The surgery is tomorrow, and I don't know what they're going to do with my eyes. They're definitely going to blind me. In fact, they want to. This is scam. He's a villain. Is he wanted by the police? Everything runs through my mind in the minute it takes him to fill my mum in on the details and we're walked out of the office.

'Even though it's hard for me to say to myself, the reality is that society does not deem me unattractive since my surgeries.'

On the way back I tell my mum I don't want the surgery. I can't trust them and anyway, I probably need to go to the hospital because all I can hear and feel is my heart trying to escape my body. She comforts me the best she can but essentially, she says 'we're here now, we're doing it'.

I don't sleep that night.

The next day we're taken to the surgery – a different building to before. Maybe this will be better. I mean, that was a doctor's consultation office, people could fuck around there all they want right? A few people are in the waiting room with us, and someone walks out with a chart and says 'WHO FIRST?'

There isn't an order?

There is no order.

This is chaos.

My heart decides it wants out.

My brother pushes me forward and I'm escorted into a dark room. Let's not forget that I already can't see, I'm not allowed to wear contact lenses in the run up to the procedure and my glasses are off. So, while I'm walked around, sat down and manhandled, I can't see what's happening. Like for example, when a thick dark liquid is poured into my eyes, and I'm told to 'keep my eyes open' despite the shock and slight burn I feel.

What I realise is that they think we're tourists and can't understand Punjabi, so there's no point telling us what's happening. We do understand Punjabi and a lot of them speak English anyway, but still ... there's no point in talking to us.

I'm then moved into the surgery room next door, where I'm laid on a bed and notice there are a few people around me. The surgeon – who I'm glad to 'see' and a few other voices. Turns out it was a couple of those pretend receptionists and the surgeon's wife. I knew it was his wife because they kept bickering about the trip, she wanted to take to Dubai that he didn't have time for. In fact, that's all they were talking about. I'm told very little about what's happening. My eyes are stretched open with an eye speculum, which causes more pain than I care to reimagine, while drops are poured into my eyes. I think of those eye drops in the waiting room the day before.

My Body Is A Temple

'Stay still darling', the surgeon takes a moment to stop bickering to say this to me before immediately slicing my cornea open. I see something come towards my eye and my instinct is to flinch. Luckily, I'm paralysed with fear, so although it felt like I was on a rollercoaster heading to my demise, I was in fact unfathomably still.

I'm told to look at the green and red light on the machine above me and to 'concentrate on the green light'. 'I'm blind AF', I think, 'I can't tell where the green light starts and red one ends'. I'm panicking again. I think about saying something and before I do the surgeon announces 'here we go!' and the laser starts shooting into my eye.

Those few seconds feel like hours, my hands are gripping onto the edge of the bed I'm on. My head isn't in any sort of vice, it's free to move and I feel like it really is. I feel like I'm headbanging to Rage Against The Machine and although I have nothing but rage now for that small machine shooting lasers at me, at the time I was in a state of inertia. Decades could pass and I wouldn't move. One day, an explorer would come to the forgotten lands of Asia and there I'd be, laying still and unmoving in a bed of dirt.

It's over.

'Up you get!'

The surgeon seems happy. Maybe I'm not blind. They instantly put sunglasses on me and tell me I should be able to see in the next few hours. I go to sit back down in the waiting room and see my brother. Maybe I should warn him. Then I remember he pushed me forward when our names were called, and I think 'fuck it'.

An hour later, I can see. It's blurry, but my sight is coming back. I push my sunglasses down every now and then to test it, but it's so bright in the Indian sun that I wince when I do. After returning to my auntie's house, I go to the

'I remember my mum
telling me ... if I sit so close
to the TV, I'll go blind.'

shaded bedroom and take my sunglasses off to inspect my bloodshot eyes and realise I can see without contact lenses or glasses.

I don't need to wear them anymore. I'm not blinded. I'm traumatised from the experience, sure. But hey, mission accomplished, right? The goal was to be glasses-free and therefore, more beautiful.

I remember when I was younger, I heard someone say 'Asians wear glasses from when they come out of their mums' and it left my mind as quickly as it entered it. But a few years after my surgery I thought of that comment. I mean, they do, right? I think of every Indian kid I know, and I can count the amount that DON'T have glasses on one hand. I remember my mum telling me that if I sit so close to the TV, I'll go blind, and I wondered if all Indian kids had a habit of making their nose touch the TV while they watch it. And did their mums say the same thing?

It was later that I found out about myopia and how it affected certain races more than others. Studies have shown that Asian countries have the highest rate of myopia, with Singapore having the highest at up to 80 per cent. In some areas, such as China and Malaysia, up to 41 per cent of the adult population is myopic and a study of Jordanian adults aged 17 to 40 found over half (54 per cent) were myopic. Research in 2017 suggested the prevalence of myopia in Indian children is less than 15 per cent. However, the 2017 research was much higher than reports before it, suggesting that there was an increase in myopia, possibly due to a competitive educational environment, long study hours and reduced outdoor activity.

When looking at European countries, another study looking at students in a UK university found that 53 per cent of British Asians were myopic. While this study suggested that despite needing a lot more research, there was no significant difference in ethnic eyes to white eyes. However, there was something to be said about how education is perceived by British Asians, causing an interest in how young people concentrate and study.

But there is a connection here. While we see less accessibility to healthcare in some South Asian states compared to others, to really see the full picture here, a big factor to the rising cases is an emphasis on studying. And I grew up with 'education is everything' hammered into me from a young age, so it sits in line.

The real issue here is the lack of evidence from recent medical trials, especially since historically, medicine was tested on people of colour, and in America, predominately Black people. For example, Black American men were used in the Tuskegee Experiment, without their informed consent, to see how syphilis (a sexually transmitted infection) worked within the body. Many of these men died despite penicillin being a known cure, because they refused to offer it as treatment. These experiments lasted for 40 years.

In India, and passed onto many immigrant families, the Ayurvedic practice of healing is the only healthcare acknowledged. It's a complex system, structured around Earth's elements juxtaposed with our bodies, and with it, a delicate balance. Unfortunately, there are all too many parts of the Ayurvedic practice that is harmful. While it is sustainable for certain health issues, it hasn't always evolved with the changing climate of the world to allow western medicine to impact it positively. For example, with treatments for cancer. Although it has also worked the opposite way – Ayurvedic treatments that are effective have sometimes been embraced by western cultures (nose jobs), and a lot of the times bastardised (yoga and meditation). It plays a complicated role in India: it's both embraced by the majority of the population, who also use a lot of western medicine.

So, in Indian families and with many PoC, there is an uncertainty in trust with western medicine, when they can use Ayuverdic or alternate methods. When we get WhatsApp messages in those horrific family groups, where they forward a video of an aunty mashing onions and garlic into a turmeric-based paste, telling you rubbing it on your belly to cure your digestion issues – maybe we shouldn't roll our eyes too hard at them. Still roll your eyes. Just not too hard.

# A broken smile

Sitting under my moustache and hooked nose was my broken smile. I don't know why I've used the past tense, it's still there. And I hate that I say 'broken smile' – it gives the connotation that it needs to be fixed. I've believed that for so long that I casually and naturally call my smile broken.

It took me a long time to laugh without my hand covering my mouth, and even now when I do, I watch people's eyes to see if they fall to my mouth. I look at people who have straight teeth with envy. Smiling is such a beautiful thing to do, and I hated doing it. I still hate it.

It's true that when you start resolving some issues in your life, others become louder. As I began to remove hair and got my nose job, I then obsessed over my teeth. I hear people say 'a woman's smile is so attractive' and I begin to rely heavily on my smile to define my beauty.

One day, on the tube with my ex, as I laughed at something he said, a man sitting opposite me exclaimed 'oh she has a missing tooth, just like me!'

My smile disappeared and I just stared at my ex, unable to move. One tooth was chipped and set back, so sometimes it looks like a missing tooth. I hated it. I hated that some random man could announce it, as if he didn't know it was something I was scared of people noticing. Why didn't he realise? I wondered if it was normal to point out people's 'imperfections' and I went further down a spiral into what an imperfection was.

## 'Because women are policed for how they look. And men can merely exist.'

I would see my body as imperfect, my face (which is misaligned) as imperfect, my hooked and then freshly broken again nose, my very existence was imperfect and so I strived to 'correct' them all.

I went on BBC Facebook Live to talk about plastic surgery and what it meant to me to get a nose job, for my mental health and especially the effects of ethnic cleansing through westernised beauty standards. The filming went well, and I felt like I had made a valid contribution. Later I read some of the comments made under the video, and aside from the expected racism, such as 'I can tell she smells of curry from here' and 'She needs to go back to where she came from if she hates it here so much', there were comments about my teeth.

'She should have gotten her teeth fixed first!'

I watched the video again and concentrated solely on my teeth. They looked horrible. I wondered whether I should get my teeth fixed. I noticed how misaligned my jaw was. No one could ever say my face has symmetry and that bothered me.

There it was.

Something new for me to obsess over.

I've been to the dentist to ask about orthodontic treatment (such as Invisalign), but after discovering the price, process and time involved with it, I asked about cosmetic fillers to plaster over the imperfections I found in my mouth. Although it's a simple process and would make it easier for me to smile without the discomfort of wondering if people are looking at my wonky teeth, I still haven't had the procedure. I'm still not sure if I should.

I don't want to find the new part of me that I dislike deeply enough to want to change.

I watch TV and question the gender bias when it comes to appearance. News presenters are the clear example of this – men tend to look however they do, as long as they're wearing a nice suit, something they can easily purchase. Whereas the women have to be slim, conventionally attractive, with perfect hair and straight teeth. I started to Google male TV presenters compared to women and would study their teeth, and almost always, the women had perfect white teeth, whereas men didn't have to. If the teeth these men had were in these women's mouths, it would be commented on. Because women are policed for how they look. And men can merely exist.

Journalist and author Alya Mooro recently tweeted: 'Someone just commented on a video of me saying I should consider getting braces!? Are people okay?????? Obviously blocka blocka blocked but like ... why the random outburst of hate? People are weird.'

I responded by telling her about my BBC Facebook Live experience and we both agreed that people have too much time on their hands. But it felt like a shared understanding. There had to be something about us that was going to be demeaned.

There needs to be a change here. Women aren't an aesthetic pleasure and should have the same balance as men when it comes to any aspect of their existence. If men can be experts on TV to discuss a report while looking however they look, so should women.

And during this, the misalignment of my jaw and wonky teeth were seen as a hindrance in finding me a match for marriage. My looks have been regularly discussed and while I was concerned about obsessing over something new about myself, I realised it was because others around me were doing it too. And I followed in their footsteps. •

# 4

# SHAME ON YOU

I'm just gonna go ahead
and be sexually liberated

The older I get, the more is expected of me. Whether it's in my career or my personal life – I am expected to succeed in the way only a woman can – and that is usually with a family. But family aside, I am also expected to have a set of values and morals that align with the older and somewhat defunct generation of women who have struggled. One thing I should definitely not be is outspoken. If any of my family is reading this book and consider it to be a horrific tale of how an Indian woman lost her way ... this is directed at you.

I've been told far too many times to keep quiet.

I've been told what I'm doing is wrong.

I've been asked why I don't have any shame.

I've been laughed at.

I've been considered uneducated and angry, instead of insightful and empowered.

All of these things echo in the lives of many people, especially for women of colour. It's unbecoming of me to talk about sex. It's unnatural for me to want to be with a woman or non-binary person. It's annoying when I talk politics. The things I say aren't true, because I don't actually know what's happening in the world.

Whether I will ever be taken seriously or not by a certain generation or family members has got a lot to do with my decisions as I age. If I don't spend this time cultivating a modest lifestyle (although modesty means having lots of money) that people can discuss with a sense of pride, then when I speak, no one cares to pay attention.

Although, as a woman, if I speak with the modesty they hope I have, they still wouldn't listen. There's no winning here. But this isn't a game, this is about people's livelihoods.

The older I get, the more I'm taken seriously, sure. But it comes at a cost. 'Okay Sharan, that's interesting, but are you making enough money? Are you thinking of buying a house yet? When will you get married? Are you too old for children now? Are you concentrating on these things and ignoring your personal life.'

And so I think ... 'am I?'

Are the decisions I'm making to try and enact change, to connect to communities and to bring people together – is that creating a larger distance between me and my personal goals? It's something I think about a lot, because I find it especially difficult to separate life and work. When examining this over the years, I came to find that there's no real difference between the two. And why should there be?

What is this 'personal life' people speak about? Is it taking time to have a long bath? Or is it about buying lots of plants for your house? Has it got something to do with the partner you choose? Maybe the number of times you see your family?

One thing I can't escape as an Indian woman is the concept of 'shame'. I am, in all manners, a shameless woman – a 'Besharam'. Hence it means someone who is not shy of anything; someone who does not think or care about the way they are perceived – more precisely, someone who is shameless. Because I refuse to live my life by a certain set of rules and expectations, I am not a good person. This means that I am not talked about in a high esteem (unless I get on TV ... although even then I've been muted, in case I was saying anything unbecoming). Instead, I'm discussed in hushed tones, where rumours start, and heads shake in disbelief.

When people gather to gossip, they say: 'Did you hear Meenu's daughter is married now to a business owner!' Maybe it's followed up with: 'Did you hear about Dhaliwal's daughter? Thirty-Seven and still not married? And she's gay? Disgusting.'

I have a very open social media rule – I don't hide my life from people because I don't believe that women should be silenced or restricted. Unless they decide to keep something to themselves, there shouldn't be any shame put on their existence. So, I talk about my mental health, my work, my sexuality, my politics and – the thing that has given me the most intense headaches – my sexual activities. In fact, I'm an avid selfie taker and in the process, I find my sexual nature shines through. Possibly just to throw in the faces of those who don't want me to, I post images of myself in lingerie, half-dressed or suggestive and I find liberation in it. It's a form of rebellion, I suppose, something I will never grow out of – but it is what has helped me figure out myself and my body. It was through social media that I found the strength to come out. It was there I built my magazine, made friendships, collaborations, found work and so on. None of these things wouldn't have happened if I wasn't unashamedly myself.

When it comes to being sexually liberated, though – that's where I've found the most pushback from my community and family. I find it funny when I think about India's sexually liberated history and fluidity, to how I'm treated for posting a selfie with a bit of underboob, to show off a tattoo.

Historically, we've had the Kama Sutra that has shown India as a sexually liberated country. As discussed in a previous chapter, India's history with sex is really complicated. Now I've talked about the Kama Sutra in a particular way, but in reality, the part of the text that looks at sexual techniques is a small section of it. A lot is about romance. It's about the importance of romance, desire and love. It's not pages and pages of sex positions other than missionary. Although those are fun to read through and at times practise (do it safely, some of these positions require some real skill and I don't have balance when I stand perfectly still), it's important to remember that the text has been viewed and translated through the eyes of a white man: Richard Francis Burton. So, the reality of the text which was compiled (maybe) sometime in 2nd and 4th century AD (so much is unknown about this including the real author), is about living well, economics, pleasure and love. What it essentially does is normalises sex within the narrative of life. Realising it's more than a 'sex book', is a lot more empowering. By allowing sex to exist alongside the philosophy of life, it refutes any shame that comes with sexual acts.

And despite this history, people will talk about sexual liberation as a moment of shame. It makes you filthy – dirty, you need to be cleaned and taught the right way. I know

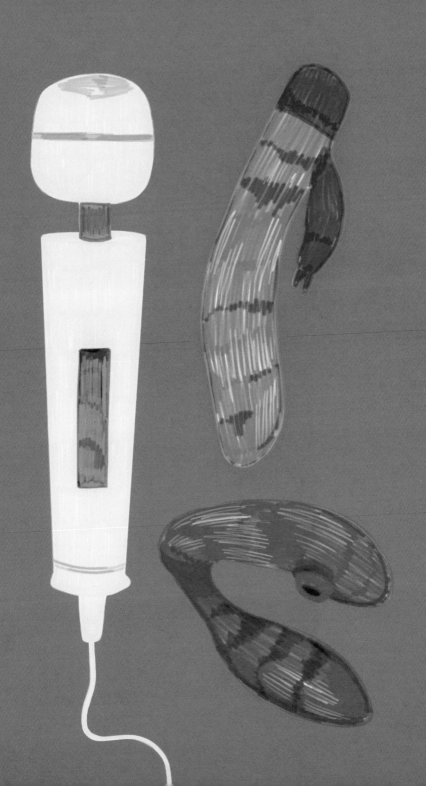

'It's not about the woman's pleasure – you must please the man enough for him to ejaculate children into you.'

that unlearning my liberation will mould me into their ideals – to conform. I don't believe I'm here to conform to anything, not only because I'm a stubborn bitch, but because I am curious. I think the reason that many people find sex to be shameful is because of the pleasure that comes with it. It's not like the pleasure of eating food, where you go 'yum, this is lovely, give me more'. An orgasm creates a full body spasm that some consider a temporary enlightenment: experiencing true nirvana. And women, well ... women aren't meant to feel pleasure. They exist truly for one reason and that's to procreate. The connection between procreation and sex is so ironic, I don't even know where to start. But yet again, it's not about the woman's pleasure – you must please the man enough for him to ejaculate children into you.

But it is also quite frankly, incredibly patriarchal. The Kama Sutra describes how to pleasure a man and although the clitoris is barely mentioned, it's rarely done in a way that is for a woman's own pleasure. It also talks a lot about caste systems, it considers certain women unworthy, it says that only 'maids' should perform oral acts, it calls some women 'smelly' and 'dirty'. Whereas men are rarely considered in this way. So even through a form of liberation, we are still unworthy.

I have been very open about the fact that I am and always will be a very sexual person. I really enjoy sex and I'm curious about it. I want to understand and learn the depths of it. I want to consider it alongside love: the difference in how that feels. I want to think about organs and ailments, and how they react to certain sexual acts. I want to think about fertility in terms of sex. But mostly, I want the autonomy to feel pleasure when I want, without someone telling me I'm not allowed. Because firstly, who are these people? Secondly, how did they come to existence without sex? Thirdly, I can't live my life according to someone else's belief structure. I refer back to the 'I'm a stubborn bitch' comment made earlier.

I'm stubborn and I'm curious. And I'm infuriated that

> ‘That’s the one thing I feel
> like have been denied –
> the ability to be curious
> at my own pace.’

curiosity has become shameful.

The thing is, you often hear people talk about a child’s curiosity with such delight, but when you hit a certain age, the delight is replaced with disgust. As soon as your curiosity questions their norms, you are no longer curious, but disruptive. A child can ask a million questions about banal things, followed by ‘oohs and aahs’ from the surrounding aunties and uncles, but when it questions something that would be considered ‘wrong’ – such as sexual preference or gender identity, instead of allowing a freedom to explore, they are ‘corrected’. This keeps happening until they believe what they are told, because why wouldn’t you trust adults?

But when you’re older, you can’t be moulded by them anymore, so they no longer feel delight in you. They definitely don’t like you. This is true for many women, and specifically for the sake of this conversation, Indian women.

## * TRIGGER WARNING: SEX WORK, ABORTIONS AND SEXUAL ABUSE *

I was exploring my body at a very young age, examining my genitals, thinking about sex and wanting to know more. The thing is, if you keep something secret from a child, they become obsessed with it. If I was told what sex was, and what it achieves, I probably would have just moved onto the next mystery.

Maybe it would have meant that I wouldn’t have slept with those really awful men, who hadn’t a clue what they were doing with their own genitals. Maybe I wouldn’t have allowed people to take advantage of me because I didn’t understand what was happening. Maybe I wouldn’t have let him continue while I cried. Maybe I wouldn't have had those abortions. Again, who knows.

What I do know is that the silence and secrecy around sex made my teenage and consecutive years, very uncomfortable. There's a misconception that being open about sex and sexual practices will mean that a young person will go forth and try it all out instantly, get pregnant, with diseases and so on. While there truly is nothing wrong with consensual sex at an appropriate age and experimentation with different bodies – telling someone about something – doesn't make them go do it with everyone. If someone told me that you could walk on your hands, I wouldn't go around walking on my hands. I'd be like, 'that's interesting, but also cool I guess.' I would think about it occasionally, watch videos of people doing it to try and understand it (unfortunately all we have in this analogy is porn and honestly, it's a mess), maybe give it a go, maybe love it, maybe decide It isn't for me, maybe think 'try again later??', but most likely keep my curiosity at an intuitive level.

That's the one thing I feel like I have been denied – the ability to be curious at my own pace. I've been told sex is wrong, shameful, embarrassing, for a husband and wife only, otherwise it's quite frankly 'disgusting' and if you practise it, you too are disgusting. And then I think back to Indian texts around sex and I wonder how people can be so openly contradictory.

Sexual liberation can be seen in many ways – whether it's accepting your body in your own personal space, whether you do sex work, or examine your sexual preferences. There are countless ways to express liberation. Some would consider sex work as being the most 'awful' way in which you could be sexually open. You are considered disgusting and dirty for charging people money for either having sex with you or merely just wanting to have sex with you. But when sex is pleasure, why should it matter? Shouldn't people search for pleasure in their lives?

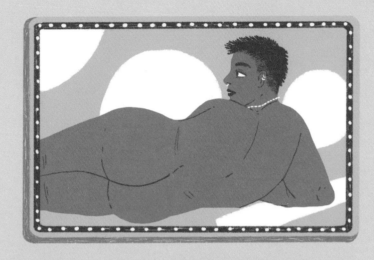

# Interview *with* Belle,
# South Asian Sex Worker

I wanted to look into the experience of others, so spoke to Belle, a South Asian femme non-binary sex worker. It took me a while to find a South Asian sex worker and especially one who was willing to speak to me about their experiences.

We are out there. South Asian sex workers exist. Femme, masculine, non-binary, queer, trans, disabled, religious, fat – we all exist in a space. The reassurance of the safety needed to exist though, is very telling. But this isn't the life for everyone – it's a stereotype to suggest that every South Asian is considerably unsafe.

'Most of my family do not know but a few of my favourite, close relatives do: my two sisters and one of my aunts. They're so wonderfully supportive' Belle tells me. I personally couldn't imagine that life myself, but then again, I haven't had that conversation with extended family. There's an inner saboteur in a sense, who tells me 'everyone will hate it'. Every action I take will be scrutinised and torn apart. Maybe it's the confidence that has been stripped from me over the years. I ask Belle about this.

'Honestly my confidence fluctuates so rapidly I don't know if you could even call it confidence that led me into sex work. A naturally thrill-seeking personality maybe? I've spent years working on self-love and acceptance and I don't know if I'm all the way there yet but I'm definitely getting closer!'

It took me a long time to find any self-love that wasn't wrapped in a man's desire. Unfortunately, my upbringing didn't allow space for that.

'I think I had quite a nuanced upbringing in terms of patriarchal influence', Belle tells me. 'There was definitely the influence of a classically Muslim household where modesty was a given but I was also given the freedom to decide whether I wanted to commit to wearing hijab and for most of my teenage years, I did. My parents really did make it clear to me that I could go on to do whatever I wanted to in terms of a career and that my gender shouldn't stand in the way of that (somehow I don't think sex work was on their list of suitable careers).' There's no shock that sex

work isn't on their list of suitable careers. Most lists have 'doctor' at the top. Surprising how many of these doctors subscribe to OnlyFans, though. The lack of education around sex for me meant that it was a difficult decision to make. Because no one would speak to me about sex, I grew up thinking it was a horrible secret. The secret being: women only did it for and with men, when they wanted and for children.

'In terms of sexuality, I was extremely lucky to have the women in my family provide me with some brilliant sex education, but it was always with the caveat that the information was to be reserved for heterosexual married life.'

But the shame is still there. It's still embedded into any messaging. Whether people are liberated or not,

'I knew that
the difference
was that he
had access to
my body and
not theirs.'

Belle

there will always be an underlying message: 'this isn't a good idea'. They don't want to hear about how that arranged marriage they organised for a woman from India was abusive and toxic, despite their celebrations during a wedding, but they will tell us about our bad ideas. This was a personal dig. Not sure if you can tell.

'I think it's disturbing and indicative of the misogyny that's built into the fabric of our society. An (abusive) ex-boyfriend once made a comment to me about some women he'd seen 'dressing like sluts' and I asked him what made me different to them since I regularly dress the same. He couldn't give me an answer, but I knew that the difference was that he had access to my body and not theirs. The same behaviour he liked in me, he was disgusted by in other women because he couldn't have them. When misogynistic men see women they can't dominate and control and have, I think it upsets them. Seeing sex work bashed hurts me in a way that feels familiar to when other aspects of my identity are attacked: my faith, my race, etc. I'm very blessed to have a network of wonderful sex worker friends who makes the whole ordeal of dealing with SWERF (Sex Worker Exclusionary

Radical Feminist) and misogynistic rhetoric a lot easier.'

Belle hits the nail on the head – men get pissed because they don't have access to women. If a random 'uncle' (I use that word loosely, we're barely ever related to our aunties and uncles) who I've never met or spoken to, tells my family that I'm posting 'lewd' photos on the internet, it's because he can't access me himself. It's because I've done something that he feels is reserved for him. So, he's angry that I'm doing it and wants me to stop. He will go out of his way to look at these images and tell people about them, instead of just putting his phone down and returning to his life. •

# * TRIGGER WARNING: CHILD SEX TRAFFICKING *

Aside from talking about shame within families, OnlyFans and the significance of patriarchal dominance over our bodies – we need to talk about exploitation. Through sex, and specifically, child sex trafficking. It's a difficult conversation to have but speaking about the autonomy of our bodies – we have the privilege over many to merely question it.

In the LSE Human Rights blog, an article entitled 'Human Trafficking in India: How the Colonial Legacy of the Anti-Human Trafficking Regime Undermines Migrant and Worker Agency', it looks into data of persons trafficked in India: 'According to data, 95% of trafficked persons in India are forced into prostitution (Divya, 2020). The recent NCRB lists a total of 6,616 human trafficking cases as registered in India, out of which trafficking for the sex trade are highest in numbers (Munshi, 2020). Since these number of cases get registered as per the definition of trafficking in section 370 that conflates with sex work, the reliability of these number thus remains contested. It is because these numbers could include cases of adult sex workers who consented, but their consent got denied during anti-trafficking interventions as both ITPA and section 370 allows it. But these figures and legislations do bring workers in sex trade into a situation of selective targeting from anti-trafficking actors and interventions (see GAATW, 2007; The Telegraph, 2017; Chandra, 2018).'

According to the National Crime Records Bureau, at least one child disappears every eight minutes in India. This is an alarming rate. I feel like people know about the child and sex trafficking that happens in India, but don't speak about it. I included. But silence isn't going to make it go away. Our inability to talk about sex supports our refusal to help those in need because of it. While sex trafficking is illegal, there is protection from corrupt police officers, who preserve brothels and exploit them for their own needs – whether it be monetary or sexual. If we don't open conversations about sex, the preservation of our bodies, male privilege and the patriarchy's control, then we can't begin to stop this from happening. It is bigger than me wanting to post a lewd photo on Instagram.

# It's about time

The story goes: 'When your brother was born, everyone came to the hospital with gifts and were so happy!!'
'Oh, that's nice,'
'They didn't come to see you. They are terrible people. This is why we don't talk to them.'
'Oh.'

I was told this story to confirm the wild ways of certain people we knew, and it was effective in that. What it also did was confirm my unimportance in the world. And as my mother gives birth to a son who is celebrated, she would have been considered unworthy for gifts when she was delivered into the world. The full circle of hypocrisy.

You are a vessel. You must be clean, perfect and unquestioning, in order to gift the world with more men.

And what do these men do? I'm yet to witness any miraculous achievements that benefit society in a positive or sustainable way. Nothing even close to the ability of creating life inside their bodies.

A lot of people hear about stories from different cultures around the world that have this unspoken (sometimes spoken very loudly) understanding that women are lesser than men, and act shocked 'oh my, that's so backwards! How awful, no no we would never.' I side-eye the pay gap, sexual assault, rape, TERFs (Trans Exclusionary Radical Feminists), workplace inequality, microaggressions, incels, abortion laws, religious ideologies and so on. It's easy to see cultures as backwards, because it means you don't have to analyse why the woman doing the same job as you, alongside being this perfect vessel, is paid disproportionately less.

I return to labour here – the word is used to excess in this book. Slave labour, child labour, work labour, enlightening labour. These are the heavy burdens of Black people, people of colour and women of colour. We are the ones who put in the work and yet we are gifted with an eye-roll for daring to exist beyond it.

While medicine has changed the way pregnancy affects people, giving them the ability to 1) actually survive it and 2) be active citizens, contributing to the world beyond carrying literal life inside them, we need to remember the intersect

'In India, for example,
we are currently
experiencing one of the
largest protests to have ever
happened on Earth. That's
a hell of a statement.'

of race here, because Black women are more likely to die
in childbirth than any other person. The sensitivity of care
for pregnant people seems to get lost in translation here, it
seems. Why is this even a statistic? Black women in the UK
are four times more likely to die in pregnancy or childbirth
than anyone else. Those from Asian backgrounds face twice
the risk. Interestingly and unsurprisingly, a lot of this has to
do with living in 'deprived areas', which is yet another reveal
of racial wealth inequality.

Covid-19 brought these statistics to the forefront with
discussions about how non-white people are treated in the
health industry, either as workers or patients. In May 2020,
I wrote an article for Prospect Magazine that looked into
this: 'As Covid-19 consumes our planet, in the UK it has
disproportionately affected those from Black, Asian and
minority ethnic backgrounds. The news is a wake-up call
to many but is met with a sombre nod of known experience
from others. Statistics this month show that 19 per cent of
deaths that have been recorded thus far are from ethnic
minority communities. Given they make up 14 per cent of
the nation's population, that's an extraordinary amount.
Just today a report from the Institute of Fiscal Studies found
that the death rate for British black Africans and black
Pakistani Covid-19 patients is more than 2.5 times than
that of the white population.'

In large cities, we see people working side by side in

'gender inclusive' environments (I'm still side-eyeing that gender pay gap, lack of opportunities for promotions and pay rises), but we forget that not everywhere is a large city with countless opportunities. We forget that some of us live in our metropolitan bubbles, where jobs come landing into your inbox as you work from home, watering an endless supply of plants and getting pastries from the French family-owned patisserie that just opened down the street.

In India, for example, we are currently experiencing one of the largest protests to have ever happened on Earth. That's a hell of a statement. I actually don't know how accurate it is, but it has been touted so by many media establishments. Either way, the Farmers' Protest is a large protest. A bit of background, without delving too deep into it and losing my trail of thought – a series of agricultural laws that were introduced in 2020 has caused protests by the mostly Sikh population of Punjab and other Northern areas of India, moving further across the land as it got bigger. Without consultation, laws were brought in that force farmers to sell crops to private firms instead of state-owned markets, heavily taxed, meaning they will see little profit. Farming employs more than 50 per cent of India's workforce, many of whom suffer from poverty and debt – so you can see the importance here.

Now bringing this back to my point, workforces are different across the world. We cannot say that all pregnant people should be treated a certain way, no matter what, because in India, a lot of the pregnant workforce works in hard labour. While in London we get maternity leave to rest, many people around the world aren't afforded that right. Not just because of gender inequality, but because of racial and wealth disparity.

And maybe that's why women's rights are discussed differently around the world. While one country wants longer maternity leave, another wants wealth inequality to stop a whole community to have to work hard labour during pregnancy.

Pictured above: Meena Kumari in *Kaajal* (1965)

I spent a lot of my youth and 20s rejecting the need to start a family. And it was a NEED, for many. Rarely is starting a family about the choice women make, instead it's their need to care and nest. When I say rejecting it, I meant I would straight up say 'ew babies, who wants that', more as a statement than a true belief. Because we all know babies are cute. I may not have wanted them, that is fine, but the outright 'ew' was a statement in how fervently I rejected it.

As a young teenager, I was taught how to make the perfect roti, for my potential suitor (a cis male). I would stand in front of the hot tavva, uncomfortable and fidgety, while being lovingly told how much flour to use. I would use too much, too little, sighing and rolling my eyes at every chance I got. I knew the reason behind this task. I didn't want to cook for a husband. I didn't even want to cook. I just wanted to eat. I watched my brother as he sits at the dining room table, reading a book, ignoring everything happening around him. And so, I would burn my rotis. It was my first effort in activism. Every roti would come out burnt or a strange shape. I knowingly knew the little patience my family held in letting me practise, so eventually, I was seated back with my brother and would await the perfectly cooked round rotis to appear on my plate.

I succeeded. Ironically, I actually now make a perfect roti. It's delicious, round and perfectly cooked, but I make them for myself. I sometimes joke that no one better tell my mother in case she rushes to get me married off now.

To be honest, I just didn't want to marry a cis man. Deep down, I knew that spending my life with a cis man would make me deeply unhappy. Especially since I hadn't yet understood and allowed myself to live my queer life. But this wasn't just about marriage. No aunty wants you to get married so you can be happy. They want you to reproduce. In fact, I know more people in unhappy marriages, than happy, who are often told to have kids in order to find that happiness they're seeking. What they're doing is bringing another human into a toxic and unhappy world. I know a lot of people in abusive marriages, who are told that it just happens, and they need to stop complaining. I know people who have been married despite the violent nature of the man they're marrying – people dance at the wedding all the while knowing the abuse the woman will experience.

It's a woman's burden.

When you reach a certain age, you no longer become a commodity. Your currency devalues until you can't be traded. An ageing woman who is unmarried usually has something wrong with her. They ask 'Why isn't she married yet? Is she too dark? Too loud? Has she had boyfriends? Is she ill?' and eventually they ask 'Will she even be able to have kids?'

I'm 37, unmarried and childless. Also, I date women and non-binary people. I am essentially a lost cause.

Although I was engaged once.

So *ahem*, I proposed to a guy I was dating. Let me explain.

In 2016, I took my partner at the time to Vancouver to meet my grandparents, and then to Portland in Oregon to see some friends. I had been dating him for a few years by then and thought the natural next move was to get married. I didn't just think it, I felt it. It was coerced into my very being. I hadn't come out yet – that would come to fruition after we break up (spoilers).

He was (and I assume is), a great guy – caring and empathetic were his strongest qualities, and I loved that. But there was something in me that wasn't okay with this. Despite that, I jumped to the conclusion that my age + that many years in a relationship = just get married.

I wasn't sure he was ready to take the leap himself. Although he was a nice guy, he was also a lazy guy, so I took the reins and bought a ring from the jewellery store next door to us. I had a plan: we would go to Vancouver to see the grandparents, therefore cementing his certainty in my life and then when in Portland, my friends and I would organise a perfect time for me to propose.

Looking back, I remember how I really wasn't that nervous about it. I knew he would say yes, but I also didn't give it the importance it deserved. Deep down, I knew it wasn't something I really wanted. When he said yes, something inside of me shifted. I exuded happiness on the outside, while a darkness grew inside me. I would talk about the wedding and not the marriage. I found myself concentrating on who would be my bridesmaids and what they would wear, over what our next steps were as a married couple. I didn't even think about what he would wear or his presence in the wedding. I distracted myself by thinking about a party and what 'fits my friends would come in.

I eventually called it off when I realised how unhappy it was making me and soon after I came out as bisexual. From then on, I felt the pressure of marriage lift off me. Not to say I won't get married, but I didn't feel like I had to. I feel a guilt that won't ever leave me, that my ex had to go through that journey with me and the outcome was painful for him. Even though I needed to be true to myself, I shouldn't have caused pain in the process. Unfortunately, it was the way it happened and I can only wish the best for him now.

The breakup led to my family going into further panic: 'she's going to have to start over, she's running out of time'. As I watch my face and body change with time, I wonder how much time I actually have to start a family.

The frustration I feel is in their reactions – as if the child that I produce will lead them into a utopia, but we all know that any child I have will be a loud, annoying, activist who will argue stubbornly with anyone who comes their way. The child will be me. I don't know, maybe not, maybe I'm

'As I watch my face and body change with time, I wonder how much time I actually have to start a family.'

projecting. And maybe that's the problem. Should I have a child? Would I even be an okay mother? I would be loving of course, I'm full of a lot of love. But will I be forceful with my politics, with my beliefs and my humanity? Does a child deserve this forceful stubbornness? Is the point in me having a child, to raise a person who will grow with trauma, like we all have?

I'm not saying that I don't want a child.

If this feels like I'm jumping back and forth between the idea of being a mother, that's because it's what the thought is like in my mind.

'At your age, people have teenage children!'

'Yeah, cool. I'm happy for them.'

And I feel my insides turn. Something inside me says 'they're not wrong' and a pain shoots across my body. It tells me it's clinging on and wants to let go. I wonder whether to tell it to let go. 'I don't want you to be a ticking clock inside me', but if I don't have a ticking clock, when will I know if it's too late?

I talk a lot about IVF – if I do become pregnant, it will most likely be with a woman or non-binary person, or on my own. I expect that I will have to go down the route of IVF for pregnancy, and that adds another element into the conversation that a lot of people don't have to have. The cost is substantial. The health issues. The trauma. The TIME. Always time. The IVF clock is also ticking.

And so I guess this is where I talk about my endometriosis and fibroids. It took until my late 20s for me to finally be diagnosed with endometriosis and a couple of years later for them to find the fibroids. Endometriosis (endo for short, I feel like I've gained a close enough relationship with it to give it a nickname) is the formation of tissue in areas that they shouldn't be hanging out in – like your fallopian tube or ovaries. It's like some tissue matter went looking for another party and chilled in the wrong place, and now won't leave, like that friend who just always sleeps on your sofa.

Uterine fibroids are a non-cancerous growth that is (also) the formation of tissue and muscle, but this time these are big ass MFs. Just a handful of them, scattered around your uterus. Basically, it seems like, the tissue and muscle in my womb had FOMO and started hanging out in areas it wasn't meant to.

Now, a lot of people don't have both – that's something I found out recently, I'm only drip-fed information occasionally because, the medical profession themselves know little about wombs. But what I have been told is that there is scarring on my fallopian tubes. This can cause issues with childbirth – but not an abnormal amount, and I could still most definitely bear a child. That was both great and awful news. Great because, if I want to pop out an activist, I can do it. Awful because now I'm thinking about it more than I normally would and especially more about the time I have.

What if my fibroids grow? What if ... and this is very rare ... but they become cancerous? My anxiety has a field day with all this.

My brother has had children and that distracts my family a fair bit. When he had his first child, I thanked my brother for the distraction and asked his wife to have the second soon after 'for my sake'. It's an added pressure I don't need from other people, because I've created enough anxiety around it myself. And while the solution is 'simple' for many – get married, have kids – it just doesn't work that way. I want to be in love, I want to be treated right, I want to feel safe, I want to know a child would also feel safe, I want to be financially stable enough to feed and clothe this child, I want to have made enough of a footprint on the world that I can spend less time writing articles about racial and queer inequality, and put that energy into playing 'the floor is lava' for hours on end with a beautiful idiot child.

I want, I want, I want.

But in reality, I only want one thing – the autonomy to choose within my own space and energy.

'When you were born, no one came to see you. They are terrible people. But, your dad was so happy. He celebrated. He bought all the ladoos and jalebi we could find and was dancing around the hospital. He's silly. He was so proud. So happy to have a daughter.' •

# 5

# ON A LIGHTER NOTE

Light skin privilege

The uncomfortable truth with India is that it fortunes lighter skin tones over those darker, and it's not subtle about it. The biggest selling beauty product in India is a skin lightening cream called Fair & Lovely, produced by the conglomerate Unilever. For those who don't know, Unilever is a multinational company, selling products from ice cream to pharmaceutical goods. They own over 400 brands including Ben & Jerry's, Marmite, Simple, Dove, PG Tips and many more, but importantly, they are the largest producers of soap in the world. They took hold of the beauty and pharmaceutical world, focusing their acquisitions on that realm, knowing that they could take control.

Hindustan Unilever, a subsidiary of Unilever, is the producer of Fair & Lovely. Although the cream is marketed and sold in many parts of Asia, it has also been exported to the West, meaning you can buy it in the UK. It's aimed at young women, of a darker skin tone, to reach the aspiration of lighter skin. The packaging itself has a before and after image of a woman with dark skin, transformed to one of lighter ... whiter skin. The controversies of this have been well documented. One I remember particularly is the use of Bollywood actors to promote this product. From Shah Rukh Khan to Priyanka 'are-you-done-venting' Chopra (Google this if you don't know the reference) – we have seen their faces on billboards and TV, telling their fans to lighten their skin. In one advert starring Bollywood actor Saif Ali Khan, you see him choose to be with a lighter skinned woman over one with a darker tone. Ironically the darker skinned woman was Priyanka Chopra herself.

(Let me interrupt my thought process here to remind you all that I have light skin privilege. I have and never will go through the discrimination faced by people of darker skin. Just wanted to say that before you all drag me.)

'It's aimed at young women, of a darker skin tone, to reach the aspiration of lighter skin.'

YOU COULD FADE AWAY *TOO!*

fair & lovely

# Interview *with* Priyanka Bose (from 2016)

In an interview with Burnt Roti magazine in 2016, Priyanka Bose, a darker skinned actor who starred in *Lion* alongside Dev Patel, as well as many Bollywood and independent films, spoke to me about how colourism has affected her career in Bollywood.

'The highest paid actors are the ones who propagate fairness creams, it's unfortunate but it's true. But for me, I don't think I'm even that brown, I'm Indian, an Indian colour: it shows how racist we are as well. The highest paid actors are white. It's not just here, it's everywhere, it's all over world. I would be signing contracts every fortnight if that wasn't true, because talent is not the issue here. It's about what family you belong to, who your friends are, and if you're not a beauty queen, your skin colour stands in the way of everything. I hope that's changing otherwise I wouldn't be able to exist!'

There are darker skinned actors out there, but sometimes, it seems that they're getting lighter every time we see them.

'There should be a revolution. The highest selling brand in India is a fairness cream brand; it's just outright racism.'

Bose is well known for starring in the 2010 Bengali film *Gangor*, as a 'tribal woman', for which she won Best Actress at the New Jersey Independent South Asian Film Festival. The film is of a photographer who goes to an impoverished village in Bengal and takes a photo of a 'tribal' woman breastfeeding her child. The photograph causes violence – she is ostracised by the village, arrested and gang-raped by the police. It centres the conversation around poverty porn and in particular, with lower caste, darker skinned women.

She isn't averse to taking controversial roles, once appearing in a jewellery advert for Tanishq as a darker skinned woman with a child, remarrying. 'I mean I was very surprised it became such a big deal; it was a beautifully done ad and I loved it for what it was,' she explains. 'The thing is, I do not sell fairness creams, I don't do the franchise that other actors do, I'm not the most expensive act as well, so because of those reasons when the Tansihq ad came out it gave it the importance it needed.'

'In 2015, when the ad came out, it was like "Oh my God, a dusky Indian woman has been cast in a remarriage advert! There's something wrong with this." The ad is gorgeous, that's all there is to it. But 'dusky' and 'remarriage' became a big thing. I know a lot of people who would love to fall in love again, with or without marriage.'•

I n June 2020, Unilever announced it was changing the name of its product from Fair & Lovely to Glow & Lovely in order to help remove connotations to skin lightening. The cream, though, contains niacinamide – which has been considered as a melanin suppressant. Which means that no matter how they go about discussing the controversy behind their product, its sole purpose is to lighten skin.

This industry has profited through years of damaging young people's self-worth. Not just Unilever, not just Fair & Lovely, but every single person who was involved in the creation of the product. And especially, every Bollywood actor who said 'use Fair & Lovely to look like me'. It's not harsh to blame these actors, you have to understand the influence that Bollywood and its stars has on the world. Not just India, but the world. Bollywood produces more films than Hollywood in any given year and ticket sales are in the billions. It's common to assume that although we are heavily influenced by pop culture around the world, it's for individuals to decipher harmful messaging. And of course, I'm not being reductive. But we shouldn't dismiss a few things here that perpetuate this so much more in places like India.

The first being the discriminatory wealth inequality that exists so openly in India. In a report by Oxfam, they discovered that 'the top 10 per cent of the Indian population holds 77 per cent of the total national wealth. And 73 per cent of the wealth generated in 2017 went to the richest 1 per cent, while 67 million Indians who comprise the poorest half of the population saw only a 1 per cent increase in their wealth.' This is an extraordinary amount of inequality. They also reported that 'there are 119 billionaires in India. Their number has increased from only 9 in 2000 to 101 in 2017. Between 2018 and 2022, India is estimated to produce 70 new millionaires every day.'

Now think of Bollywood as one of the biggest money-making businesses in India – the glamour of the industry is for the poor to aspire to. It's evident in some of the stories in Bollywood films themselves: in *Om Shanti Om*, an epic about reincarnation and love (literally the longest three hours of my life), Shah Rukh Khan is a poor man who aspires to be a Bollywood actor and marry the biggest actor

> '*Bollywood has been a leading marketing solution for skin lightening creams, with a lot of actors since coming out with apologies for being part of those campaigns.*'

at the time – played by Deepika Padukone. In many stories, a poor man or woman wants to marry a rich person they fall in love with, but the family object. It's for aspiration. 'You may be poor, but you can marry into wealth'. But the reality is far from these romanticised tales, where these love stories lead to violence and sometimes death.

The aspirations reach beyond love and into beauty ideals – the women are always fair, thin, hairless and multilingual. In comparison to the men, who tend to be darker skinned, don't fit into most standards of beauty and are 'rascals'. Yet these women yearn for these men. They are unattainable in reality but in these films, they are the standard. So, these beliefs bleed into the real world, where men believe any woman belongs to them, and every woman should meet a standard of perceived 'perfection'. Marriage is the clincher here and it allows men to enact violence in their power through ownership. When I say violence, it's on all levels – from domestic violence, to preserving unattainable ideals as the norm.

Bollywood has been a leading marketing solution for skin lightening creams, with a lot of actors since coming out with apologies for being part of those campaigns. When sending out tweets for support of the Black Lives Matter protests in 2020, many Bollywood stars faced backlash for their incessant promotion of products such as Fair (Glow) & Lovely. The star of one of my favourite Indian films (*Fire*, made in 1996, because surprise surprise it's about two women who fall in love), Nandita Das, has said she faced discrimination in the industry. In an article in the Guardian titled, 'Glamour, glitz and artificially light skin: Bollywood stars in their own racism row', written by Alia Waheed, Das says: 'The glorification of fair skin has been present in our films for a very long time and reflects the bias of our society.' She continues: 'When I play a slum dweller or a Dalit (untouchable caste) woman, my skin is perfect, but directors tell me to make my skin lighter to play affluent upper-class roles.'

'Films associate fairness with beauty, success and love and acceptability. It becomes about making women feel inadequate. It's hypocritical to protest and say #blacklivesmatter, yet discriminate against people with dark skins and endorse fairness products in our own country. Now society is more vocal about these hypocrisies and many actors have been called out for it. The more we call out discrimination, the more we address the issue.'

## * TRIGGER WARNING: NEGATIVE DEPICTIONS OF BLACK FOLK *

In the film *Fashion* (2008), Priyanka Chopra plays an aspiring fashion model who experiences alcohol and drug abuse. But it was in one scene, where she sleeps with a Black man that was considered her lowest point.

In the 1969 film *Intaqam*, during the song *Aa Jaane Jaan*, renowned dancer Helen performs a song around caged men in blackface. Helen herself is incredibly light skinned and wears a blonde wig and coloured contact lenses to really contrast against these painted men.

In the 2020 film *Khaali Peeli* (the literal translation is Black Yellow, and refers to taxi cabs), a song called *Beyoncé Sharma Jaayegi* (translates to 'Beyoncé will be ashamed', in a demure shy way, I suppose), that particular line was removed from the original when it faced backlash for being racist. The song states that the leading lady in the film is so fair skinned, that even Beyoncé would be ashamed. While the writers said 'no offence was intended', it's difficult to see how. In an industry where racism and colourism are the foundations it has been built on, we see why it happened, but not why it continues to. Let us not

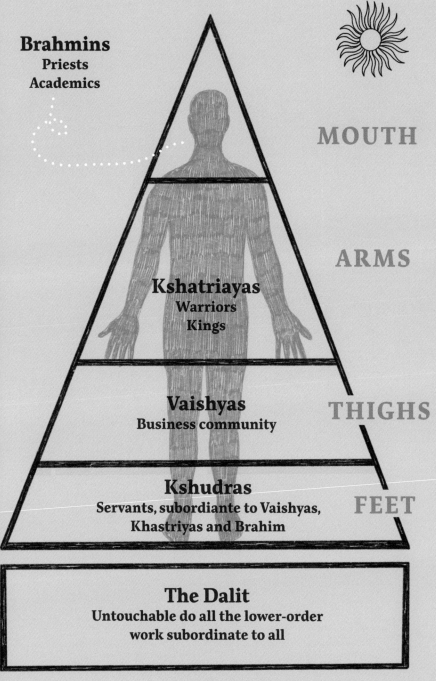

**Brahmins**
Priests
Academics

MOUTH

**Kshatriayas**
Warriors
Kings

ARMS

**Vaishyas**
Business community

THIGHS

**Kshudras**
Servants, subordiante to Vaishyas,
Khastriyas and Brahim

FEET

**The Dalit**
Untouchable do all the lower-order
work subordinate to all

Illustration above: The caste system of India

'The depths
of caste violence
runs in our land,
politics and
people: in India's
and England's.'

forget that the industry is also built by and controlled by men. So, while these ideals of fairness are problematic for women, the men of the industry continue to profit from it.

A song I would regularly sing as a young woman 'ye kaale kaale ankhen, ye gore gore gaal' (your black, black eyes, your white white cheeks), from *Baazigar* starring Shah Rukh Khan and Kajol, later became more than just a fun song, when I realised what I was saying. Ironically, the star of the film Kajol was considered darker skinned than most, but had light (green) eyes, so attained to a component of whiteness others did not. But the song didn't make sense. Her eyes were green.

Anyway. The list goes on, there are countless times Bollywood has perpetuated the ideals of whiteness through fair skin. Although everything is interconnected – wealth, the media and also the division of labour, stripping them down into individual talking points means we can understand where they came from.

The caste system in India is structured by your job – teachers at the top, street sweepers at the bottom. While the higher caste tends to be of lighter skin, the lower are darker and work outdoors. This story is known in African slavery, when Black people were taken to the fields to work tirelessly, while white people would sit in their sheltered homes, looking on and drinking iced tea. Darker skinned people would only marry other darker skinned people and so on, so the division continued.

Okay, so let's talk about the caste system. The most well-known system is the Hindu hierarchy of Brahmins at the top, followed by Kshatriyas, Vaishyas, Shudras and at the bottom, the Dalits. These categories are formed from labour duties: Brahmins tend to be priests and teachers, whereas Dalits are street sweepers. There is a lot of discussion around the conception of caste systems, and no matter how much I like to say how brilliant I am, I'm no historian, so am unable to really pinpoint its inception.

But what I do know is that it was prevalent before the British rule.

In the Mughal Empire, royalty were the highest caste members, and it was here that a lot of inequality was established. Not the start of the caste system, I must add – as I said, I'm not sure about the true beginnings of it.

On A Lighter Note

It was during the British rule that it was perpetrated to a degree that was an established way of life – in the sense of 'administration'. Yeah, you read that right. The British perpetuated the caste system for admin needs.

Using the caste system, the British appointed jobs to those only of higher castes and furthering division. They then applied laws that only affected people form lower castes. They stated that those from lower castes were born with criminal tendencies and introduced the Criminal Tribes Act of 1871.

Now, the reason this is discussed in this chapter – those of lower caste tend to have darker skin. Strict marriage rules (only marry those within your caste) have sustained this, but the reason can also be seen in labour and wealth. Those in lower castes would work outside and have no access to shelter. We can never discuss colourism without talking about the caste system, colonialism and wealth inequality.

So what, this was ages ago in India. How does it affect anyone now?

Well, it isn't history. The caste system has not magically disappeared, wealth inequality is strong and the political landscape of Hindu Nationalism cements it. India's prime minister Narendra Modi is the leader of the Bharatiya Janata Party (BJP), which is known for its right-wing policies, reflecting Hindu nationalist positions. Hindu Nationalism is considered as the idea that being a true Indian is to be Hindu.

Okay but how does it affect YOU, Sharan?

Good question. It doesn't because of my privilege. But it still affects darker skinned and lower caste folk who have emigrated to different countries. We must remember it is the British who perpetrated these caste systems into administration roles for the benefit of their rule. We can't expect people to come to the land that did that and not to still feel the harsh violence of caste divides. But it is also within the community itself, because while they left India for new land, they didn't leave their beliefs. In 2010, research was completed by the Government Equalities Office on caste discrimination and harassment in Great Britain: it considered discrimination covered by the passage of the Equality Act 2010 in relation to: work (bullying, recruitment, promotion, task allocation);

provision of services; and education (bullying). A line that stood out from the report for me was: 'At the extreme, caste prejudice and harassment resulted in violence.' It suggests that there is discrimination in all these aspects, as well as the voluntary sector, religious groups and public spaces and that it should be addressed.

There has since been another report on caste-based discrimination in 2017, that was used to ask the government to add caste-based discrimination into the race section of the Equalities Act 2010. According to Parliament's open-source website: 'The consultation was published on 28 March 2017 and ran until 18 September 2017. The Government published its response on 23 July 2018, concluding against further legislation, preferring to rely on developments in case law. The Government has therefore committed to repealing the duty, under the amended section 9 of the Equality Act, to legislate to prohibit caste discrimination.' They said 'nah'. So technically ... it's legal, under the Equalities Act 2010, to discriminate against people for their caste. Great Britain, indeed.

I won't fill these pages with how I was told to stay away from the sun, or how I was considered eligible for marriage due to the lightness of my skin. This only furthers the trauma experienced by darker skinned women and non-binary people. When discussing colourism, with my light skinned privilege, it's definitely not about me or my direct experiences pertaining to being light-skinned. And although this book is about my experiences, this subject is too important and too often ignored by people who look like me, to not discuss.

We must also remember that the caste system isn't solely applicable to the Hindu faith. My family are Punjabi Sikhs and whilst Sikhism teaches us about equality away from caste systems, the cultural society is run from a system that puts people in a hierarchy, with Jatt people (land owners) being the highest caste. I would walk around stating 'yeah I'm a Jatt' proudly, solely because it rhymed with 'butt' and I thought I was hilarious. But the connotations were that I was better than anyone who wasn't a Jatt, and whether I understood the meaning behind it or not, I knew deep down that there was something 'good' about being a Jatt, compared to any other caste.

On A Lighter Note

# Interview *with* Mum

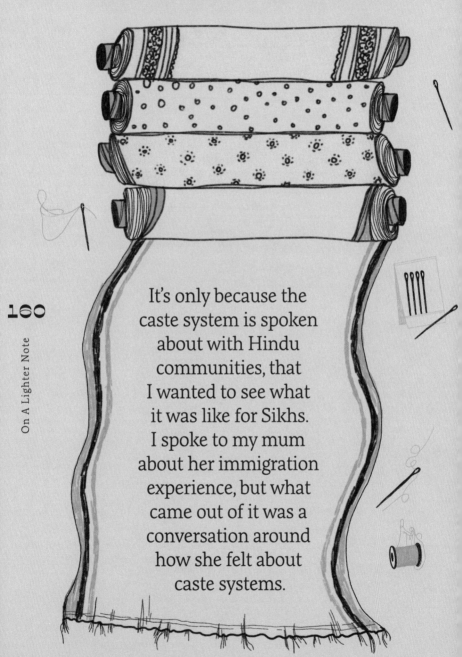

It's only because the caste system is spoken about with Hindu communities, that I wanted to see what it was like for Sikhs. I spoke to my mum about her immigration experience, but what came out of it was a conversation around how she felt about caste systems.

Although her immigration experience is important, it is only through rose-tinted glasses, as – she herself said: 'I came from a place of privilege'. We delved into that privilege with stories about how she grew up.

But first, she remembered something she wanted to tell me.

'When you were a young child – around three years old – we went to Broadway Southall to get clothes and there was another lady there waiting to be served. She was Indian as well and she had a daughter who was very fair-skinned – she was about two or three years older than you, I think. You started talking to each other and playing, and I was talking to the lady. When we were coming back and you were in the car, I saw something happened – the girl threw something at you. I just ignored it and you were quiet but then, when we were sitting in the car you said to me "Mum" and I said "what Sharan?" and you said "you know that girl hit me?" I said "why Sharan?" and you said "because she has a white face and I had a brown face" and I said "Sharan,

maybe she had a white face but she had a dark heart". I remember that. Certain things you remember.'

I do not remember that. I don't remember any of that story but to be honest, we were taken to Southall Broadway on a weekly basis, and I'm not sure how often things like this happened to me.

I mentioned how I'd like to speak to that girl now (If you're reading this, email me). Mum laughed, she thought back again to those days and considered how things were so strange when it comes to lightness of skin, but she had experienced it herself. I would never consider my mum as dark-skinned but in her family, she was.

'I wasn't light-skinned. My sister was. I was told I was dark compared to her. She was the favourite because she was lighter skinned. I was considered dark, and therefore less desirable.'

My masi is lighter skinned and my nani was also very light skinned, which my mother said she got from her father. I consider bringing up where Nani's light skin comes from and if back in our ancestry, some people were having sex with people outside of India. I decide not to broach that today. Maybe another day.

We started talking about the village and her life there. She took a deep breath before carrying on and I could tell, from everything we spoke about, this was the hardest.

'In our house the caste system was so bad. We used to have buffalos in the house and also, every house had a dedicated one low caste family who would look after you. There was one for us as well. They used to come in the morning and stand outside our house, queuing up for milk from the buffalos and I wasn't allowed to speak to them. Because what happened is, one day I touched their milk pan to our milk pan and oh my god, everybody shouted at me. And they said she has "no akal" (common sense), you're not meant to touch our pans. I remember that old lady. She used to work in our house all day long and when it happened, she said "no child, don't do that, don't touch our pans, don't worry, I'll pour out the milk". It broke my heart.'

Mum tuts an goes quiet for a bit. I fill the silence with how it's still so prevalent and it's so sad to see it happen. I tell her about how it transmits into life in England too.

'I was totally against it and I was the only one. I was treated like a villain in the house. One day I went to their house – they were so happy that this girl from a higher caste house came round. They made sabji (a veggie dish) for me. I ate roti there and everyone went after me for going there and eating. And I was like "what's wrong with that?

## 'I was considered dark, and therefore less desirable.'

you know?" I was totally against it. From day one, I have seen people in India doing that. They're still doing it so much'.

I think the problem here is not just that people treat those of lower caste in such a way, but that the system itself exists to allow mistreatment and even no matter how many times we look back at how it was 'worse' or 'different', the problem is... it's still there.

'That really breaks my heart. That woman's one daughter, the young girl – she's is in Belgium and I went to see her. She was over the moon that I came to visit. Even her children. One was holding up a towel and another slippers at me when I came

through the door. They were treating me like I'm a queen because I was visiting them. And they are so well off, they own lots of properties and are living a good life. But it's still inside them'.

That's what we mean with a trauma that never leaves you. It's been ingrained inside them to treat others a different way, so much so that those who are mistreated are unable to live any other way. When my mum visited, they weren't just being great hosts because it brought memories for my mum of how she was treated in the village in comparison to them. Even her children, a different generation, were abiding by this caste system. That's the reality of these systems. •

● n 2015 and 2016, a campaign launched online called #UnfairAndLovely, which showcased dark skinned women, rejecting light skin ideals and celebrating their beauty. Although it's regularly erased, the project was started by Pax Jones, a non-binary Black femme photographer. In an interview with *Teen Vogue*, Pax Jones said: 'Systems of oppression work with each other … Each system affects the other, so people existing at the intersection of these oppressed identities need to be protected and celebrated more than ever. The intersection of identities makes it absolutely pertinent for everyone to make an active effort to dismantle systems of oppression.'

The inspiration to start their photo series came from a friend – a South Asian woman who had similar experiences of colourism: 'I was mainly interested in exploring the intersections of colourism, going between my own black experience and her South Asian, specifically Tamil, experience,' they say.

There's irony in the fact that a Black non-binary person was excluded by South Asians on a conversation about colourism. While we centre ourselves, we have silenced Black voices.

In an interview with *Daily Dot*, Jones confronts this: 'My biggest issue is when I read any sort of article and the centre of it was this movement for dark-skinned South Asian women. Not only was that misinformation, but it carried over to other places.' They continue: 'I remember very distinctly seeing someone having a conversation saying, "Why are Black girls trying to come into this hashtag? You guys already have #BlackGirlMagic, you already have this, you already have that, this isn't for you." And when I saw that, I was just like, "OK, well, this is over with."'

Jones had to later step away from the project, 'People, especially Black femmes for whatever reason, always have to remind themselves that they did do the work. Even though people are going to convince us that we didn't.'

A year later, Jones decided to reclaim the hashtag, by hiring a lawyer, trademarked the hashtag and relaunched the movement to be inclusive of all dark-skinned people, including Black people, instead of centring South Asians. They told *Daily Dot*: 'The target is all people of colour who have the potential to experience colourism. We view colourism as a global phenomenon.

# 'There is a fine line between giving people a platform and taking it for yourself.'

We want the reach to be global.'
While we discuss light skin privilege, colourism and the caste system ... anti-blackness is an important conversation here.

In 2020, *Burnt Roti* released Issue 3 on anti-blackness in South Asian communities. The idea came about years before and I had contacted the cover stars in November 2018, asking about their thoughts on doing this issue and how they felt about having the discussion. It was a group of mixed race Black and South Asians creatives who I wanted to profile and give a chance to express their particular experiences. After a long process of funding issues, mental health problems and personal spanners being thrown in the works, *Burnt Roti* managed to publish it in 2020.

There is a fine line between giving people a platform and taking it for yourself. You see that in the behaviour of white people who stand up to racism, usually to take the spotlight and revel in their activism. This also happened with #UnfairAndLovely and many other movements. Whether the intention is to be supportive or not, there can be a feeling of white saviourism. (The use of 'white' is more about the proximity to white supremacy and privilege than it is an actual skin colour.)

Without disregarding the work historically done by South Asians or the very real anti-racist activism that has brought significant change, and especially without disregarding the notion of privilege within the area of South Asia – with Northern Indian Punjabis (such as myself) having more privilege than for example those in Bangladesh who face a different kind of discrimination – the print issue was created to help carry on the conversation.

Whether it managed to sit beyond the line of saviourism is something to be considered, because it yet again, came from a place of privilege. The Jatt light-skinned Punjabi

165

British-born woman creating an issue on anti-blackness huh? The attempt was to bring the focus away from myself, from the usual conversations about marriage and ideals, and into the stories of those ignored. We spoke to Black students in India about their experiences, we had Black writers discuss certain experiences, we introduced ideas on how to be a workplace ally and showcased photo campaigns of Black communities living in India.

My personal experiences have not been affected by the lightness of my skin, but from the inception of this issue. I questioned whether it came from a place of guilt. Like, white guilt. White tears. My proximity to whiteness forced this conversation out of me. There's nothing wrong with admitting that I regularly drag myself: while yelling 'oh the racism!!' I think 'yeah, but how have I perpetuated it' and it's no longer that voice in the back of my head, it's at the forefront. Through years of allowing my privilege to dampen any acknowledgement in my involvement, I finally began to bring it out.

Individually, we all need to do this work, but it isn't just through statements and producing print issues – it's through learning and understanding. We lack empathy as a race, and with knowledge, we will gain more. When we refuse to learn why something affects people, we don't just ignore them, but we ignore a large part of our humanity.

We've seen Palestine endure a decades-long war of colonial settler organisations demolishing whole neighbourhoods, arresting and torturing children, while murdering families. People around the world are very aware that something is happening. 'There's always a war around there, is it about oil?' I've heard people say. Only until recently, through the help of social media have we begun to pay attention. We watched videos, heard voices, and looked on as Israeli soldiers tore people apart. We began to learn, through shared information and because we can't ignore those pained screams, our humanity kicked in.

The challenge is to no longer wait for people to scream so loudly we can hear them, in order to pay attention. The point is for us to want to help people all the time, because we are clued in. We know what's happening and we want to help. Stay informed, stay prepared.

'When we refuse
to learn why
something affects
people, we don't
just ignore them,
but we ignore
a large part
of our humanity.'

# I'm not your preference

Oh boy, here we go. How many dates have you been on where your race was brought up? Actually, how many times was it brought up at work? I was sitting in an office on my second week there and the manager at the time said:

'I'm going on holiday; I hope it isn't too sunny. I mean, I want to tan but not that much. I want to get to Sharan's skin colour.'

I stopped (pretending I was) typing and froze. I was unable to look up from my laptop. I could hear the heaviness of the silence fill the room. A nervous laugh followed. Furious typing followed closely after. The silence had to be filled somehow. Eyes were on me.

There's a couple of things here. I was the only person of colour on the team, in a predominately white organisation, who – to be clear – hired mostly South Asian people in order to hit their diversity quota. But within my team, I had no one to give 'the look' to. You know, the 'what did they just say' look. I was alone in this feeling. While there was sympathy in the eyes I could feel on me, there was no real understanding. No one there knew the feeling of being called a p*ki in a pub, of being profiled in airports, or being told they smell of certain foods. No one understood that although my manager wanted to tan to my colour, their tan would wear off and I would still be this colour. And importantly, that my skin colour isn't what creates racism, but the way people view my culture. So even if my manager reached my skin colour, they wouldn't receive any of the discrimination I have faced. In fact, their skin would be praised: 'wow, you're glowing!' people would exclaim, while they smugly announce they want to use tanning beds to keep 'the glow.'

The glow.

They glow and we are a burden.

I was new in the job, so I didn't feel like I could say anything, out of fear of being ostracised or possibly given a warning. When people speak up on racism, they aren't usually given a medal for it. You're guilt-tripped into thinking you talk too much about race that you victimise yourself. That people are not being mean, they are in fact being kind. Wanting my skin tone is a compliment!

And with it, you centre the other person's feelings. You think, 'I don't want them to feel uncomfortable around me.' Or 'I don't want people to think they said something really bad.' You think 'I just want to do my job, get paid and go home to bitch about them.' This allows these conversations to continue. Who knows how many other people are harmed by this person's reckless comments – people more vulnerable than me. You shrug the comments off your shoulders and onto those who wear a heavier burden.

'It was a throwaway comment!' and 'they didn't mean anything by it!' follows days after, invalidating my feelings of being othered. They throw that comment out into the world, carelessly and with abandon. Meanwhile, years later, I think about it so much, I'm writing about it in this book.

It's not that this was the worst experience I've ever had, but it was a turning point for me. I realised how uncomfortable I was with my silence, and it led me to face that. I began to learn to centre myself instead of others. I noticed more and more in that job that I was underpaid compared to my cis white male counterparts, who I was doing an extortionate amount more than in my work. I was told I went on too many smoking breaks. No one else was told. Not even the white team members I would go with. I was given negative reviews despite my workload causing mental health issues to spiral even more. Meanwhile, others on my team would spend their day playing ping pong and sending messages on social media group chats about how bored they are.

Work environments aside, I've had people engage with my race while dating. Not in a positive way, but in a way that fetishises me. There was a woman, (yes, you guessed right, she's white), who I went on a couple of dates with and my friends and I still speak about her actions to this day. I came across her on Twitter and we started talking over DMs. She showed mild interest, but not as much as I did: remember, I was eager to prove my bisexuality with women and non-binary people, so would find myself engaging excessively on social media platforms. We eventually exchanged numbers and went out on a date. On the lead up to the date, I would receive a flurry of messages, showing interest but also a very specific interest. She talked a lot about Bollywood and well ... Indian things.

At one point, assuming she knows more than me, would tell me things about the Bollywood stars I grew up with. I assumed she was just dense, but my horniness took over and I went on the date. It was awkward: she controlled a significant part of the conversation and as it was my first proper date with a woman, I was nervous. The date ended and I felt strange. A few days later we were still talking over text, and she kept talking about India and I found myself sighing every time her name popped up on my phone.

I was on the bus, coming back from a meeting when I looked at my phone and saw a message saying:

'I'm obsessed with Indians now. Watching these movies like "CAN I HAVE ONE?"'

I stopped moving. In fact, it felt like the bus had stopped in shock too. It felt like everyone on the bus took a sharp intake of breath and were staring at my phone.

'CAN I HAVE ONE?'

Can I have one? My mind goes to takeaways, because I always give people the benefit of the doubt. She's hungry for a takeaway? No, she wasn't. She was hungry for an Indian person. The cannibal nature of her fetishisation is not an exaggeration – there's a need to devour the culture, the people, the art. They consume it.

'Indian people fucking love me. I will be in an item song. I WILL BE.'

Do Indian people fucking love you? Really? Because this Indian person is really regretting that date. For those who don't know: an item song is a number in a Bollywood film, performed by a dancer/actor who isn't cast as a main character but is just introduced for this song – and it is usually very seductive. Like a sexy cameo that no one needed. I guess that sums her up as well.

'I FANCY ALL INDIANS. Hahahahahahaha!'

The laugh was deafening.

She talked about adopting an Indian accent, about learning how to speak and write in Hindi and then perform her stand up (yup, she's a comedian). She talked about wearing Indian dresses like they were costumes and has since modelled for Pakistani TV. She would send me scribblings of her learning Hindi and ask me to translate certain words.

I'm Punjabi. I know Hindi from Bollywood. Also, I can barely write in English, I can't decipher what you're writing,

'She was not
at all interested in
me, my personality,
my work, my looks,
my desires ...
she was interested
in the fact that
I'm Indian.'

woman. Eventually, I stopped replying more and more. It took longer than it should have because my heart was broken over the idea that my first proper date with a woman went down like this. What were the chances. I was so adamant that men were the worst and then I was reminded that white women are not far behind them. She was not at all interested in me, my personality, my work, my looks, my desires ... she was interested in the fact that I'm Indian. She didn't care that I had a magazine that works with creative and young people. She didn't care that I wanted to talk about systematic oppression. She definitely didn't care about any of my stories. She didn't even really want to be with me in any sense of the word.

She wanted to use me to learn how to be more Indian. This white woman. Turns out she was known in the comedy circuit for being problematic and my friends who were actual good comedians filled me in. I've been fetishised by men before, but that's kind of expected. I have very little expectation from them, so I wouldn't be surprised. But when it came from the first woman I went on a proper date with, it sent me down a hole of uncertainty. I wasn't sure whether I was able to survive the dating world as a bisexual person, because men suck and now, I had this awful experience. So, what now?

Through time and speaking to others, I developed confidence back in myself, but it has still stuck with me. Now when someone says 'I'd like to watch a Bollywood film with you', after I've told them I've spent the whole day dancing to Bollywood songs, instead of saying 'sure!', my mind thinks 'okay but why though'. And I scrutinise actions. I rarely give the benefit of the doubt. I often overanalyse.

If a white partner mentions children my mind instantly thinks 'yeah, you just want mixed babies', instead of 'aw cute, but no thanks'. It's not just off the back of this experience, it's from years of seeing it happen around me. I've mostly witnessed these comments and attitudes from white people to Black people, because the fetishisation of mixed babies from them is at the absolute highest. They want the exotic elements of a different skin tone, but with

On A Lighter Note

the European features that align to beauty standards. Not too dark, nose still small, eyes light and so on.

This tells people of colour that they are good enough to have sexual intercourse with, but their features and skin still need to align to whiteness in order to be palatable to wider society – that people of colour, and specifically women in this case are here yet again, to procreate a new race of humans. There's an urgency to mix ethnicities with white, to get a light brown mix of people, eroding whiteness completely, but only from skin tones. This doesn't erode whiteness as a concept but instead amplifies it. It's still saying that darker skin needs to be lighter to be the norm (in this new light brown utopia).

Anyone can and should have children with whoever they want, no matter their gender, sexuality, race, caste or religion. It's not a remark on mixed relationships and their ability to procreate through love and family – it's the intention that needs to be discussed. If people are having children just for an aesthetic, then that child is being brought up to be fetishised, instead of being allowed to simply exist. There are regular posts on Twitter and Instagram, of people fawning over mixed children, for having lighter skin and eyes, and comments that say 'they're going to be so beautiful!' or 'wow look at their eyes!'

That makes me uncomfortable. When an eight-year-old Afgani student named Sharbat Gula was on the cover of the *National Geographic* in 1985, her light eyes made her the topic of discussion. We know if her features were traditionally darker, people would not be interested in her story. The caption read 'Haunted eyes tell of an Afghan refugee's fears'. I thought of the haunted eyes of all refugees who weren't as important as her. I found her beautiful too, and as a child I also wanted light eyes. I believed they would make me more beautiful. I knew if I had my skin and light eyes, I would be revered, almost like a circus performer on stage, ogled by the masses. I knew I would be considered more interesting and whiteness would fall easier at my feet. I would be the preference.

Too often it's been asked 'is it racist to have a sexual preference?' and I can absolutely tell you that yes it is. An ex once told me 'I've fucked an Asian now'.

'What?', I was genuinely confused.

'I've ticked off all the races! Haha! You were the last one!'
I tried not to laugh but I did, and it was at the absurdity of the comment.

I was a tick box. Not just at work, in social spaces, on panel talks, on the TV, but also in the loving relationship where I wanted to feel safe. He was happy at how anti-racist he was by sleeping with women from all the ethnicities he knew (not many) and it left me feeling insignificant. I have heard the 'I haven't had an Indian' (usually followed by 'except a takeaway!! Wheey!!') comment far too many times to recount them all. It's not just said by men trying to flirt with me, it's used in 'casual jokes', which remind me of those moments. A white person at work has previously made a conscious decision to make a remark on my ethnicity and dating life.

'Indians' date white people?'

Did you all know that anyone can date whoever they want to? That's right, this book is full of extraordinary revelations like this.

I think people assume my family wouldn't let me be interested in, date or marry anyone other than a Sikh Punjabi man and you know, this whole book is me telling you that it's what has been forced onto me, so... fair. But the connotation from a white person, with no real knowledge of the nuance, of the influence of the British, of the tragedy in our history, of the distrust – no white person should have an opinion on the matter. I can already hear it, 'God, we can't say anything can we?' Correct.

No okay I'm joking, you can. But think about it before you say it. Would you ask your white friend if they date Indians, or would you nod and congratulate them on their apparent anti-racist activism by merely dating a person of colour? Would you tell your white crush that you're into them because of 'fish and chips', or would 'cultural' food have nothing to do with it? (Fish and chips are apparently Not Even British. I can't deal with this information, but I've been told that it originates in many forms across Spain, Portugal and Holland before making it to British shores.)

Ask yourself: why is it so important to you to have to mention my race at all and especially ... so negatively? You can consider my existence as an Indian woman, without the shackles that tie me down because of it. •

# 6

# HOLD THEM TO ACCOUNT

White people ... am I right??

We're standing on the main stage and RuPaul pulls out a photo of me when I was young. It's held up in front of me, in full view and I stare at the strained smile on my hairy face, with thick glasses and large nose.

'What would you say to young Sharan?', RuPaul enquires.

While holding back tears, I respond.

'Nothing.'

I wouldn't tell myself anything, because despite any regret I do have, or any hopes and wishes, we don't live in a world that would allow me for a different upbringing. There is nothing I could have done to change my journey: it's not my fault.

Maybe that's what I will say, actually. I do want to make the top four and impress RuPaul and I don't think saying 'nothing' will get me anywhere. While I want to admit that there have been so many things in my life that were built against me, I don't want to be silent about it, because the point is for change. And while we work on changing our views on how we love ourselves, we need to hold them to account. The institutions, the media, the colonisers, the wealthy, the whiteness – and instead of whispering, from fear of experiencing accusing eye-rolls, we will say it out loud.

Now, I'm not saying we shouldn't work on ourselves. We have a lot to do. As a privileged middle class, light skinned cis Punjabi Indian woman – I can't sit here and say 'boooo! The Brits!!' about literally everything (I know, I know, stay off my Twitter), because I personally benefit from their systems. I benefit from my name sounding white. My body, albeit in pain, is an 'acceptable weight', colour and shape. I conform (I suppose) to gender roles in many ways. I'm not poor. So, I must examine my actions and thought process with what I do. Importantly, I don't blame myself for my thin body. I don't further punish myself – I am aware of the standards that have been passed to me that cause the trauma. So, I hold them to account, while being careful not to victimise myself. I'm not that emo 16-year-old listening to Marilyn Manson (also hold him to account for sexual abuse claims) anymore.

'While I want to admit that there have been so many things in my life that were built against me, I don't want to be silent about it, because the point is for change.'

I can look at my body and feel pain and trauma, but I can look outwards and see why it happened. At the same time, I can see where I benefit from the system. It's not a difficult thing to do, our minds are able to process more than one thought and even though we like to irk towards selfishness, there's a sense of ego in recognising this – so it hits those levels too.

The beauty in holding them to account is that you can't help but look within yourself because we have had to absorb whiteness as an ideal. So, you can't shake your finger at whiteness without turning it onto yourself and with an element of shock, horror and surprise, to tell yourself off too. Not in a harmful way – you don't need to oppress yourself further, but mindfully consider your actions. While being generous to yourself, you examine your life. When I say there is 'beauty' in it, it's because the revelations become unceasing.

'Yeah but because of colonialism, right?' is now part of almost every sentence. And even though (as I've said previously), it's nice to blame everything on colonial histories, it's also important to see how communities have benefited from it.

'Yeah but because of colonialism, right? That's why colourism is such an issue?' – yes, it is. But as we've discovered, colourism existed before the British exacerbated it. So maybe it's: 'Yeah but because of colonialism, right? That's why colourism is such an issue? Because the 'white' mindset existed before they came to India and we are susceptible to the concept of white supremacy, maybe that's why when they left, it didn't leave a lot of us.'

# How to hold them accountable

## 1.

## Don't Keep Quiet

I've been told to be quiet one too many times. With being a woman comes silence and shame. In order to placate us, they control us. Okay this sounds like a strap-line to some gender-flipped *Die Hard* film. Let me try again.

There's an expectation that women will just deal with what life offers them, but we know that life is offering them little and for the benefit of men. So the expectation is a false hope and we can squash this narrative by speaking up. One thing I have struggled with and continue to is the uncomfortable nature of speaking about harm. Whether it's saying 'white people' or 'anti-blackness' or 'gendered violence', there tends to be pushback from people to silence you. The uncomfortableness is theirs, not yours. Don't let people think 'there's a time and place to talk about things' because those times and places don't exist for you, it's for their comfort. We shouldn't wait for them to sit down, take the weight off their feet and grab a cup of tea, because we haven't been given that privilege. When you speak up and people react in a way that makes you feel shame – it's usually because you've said something important.

The best thing I've done is remove all egos from the conversation and said what is needed to be said. Now, I have the privilege to do so. This isn't to say 'everyone should say everything all the time', because some people are in the direct path of violent harm and shouldn't have to prod that harm with an iron stick.

Use your privilege to dismantle that harm that stands in their way, and you can do that with your voice.

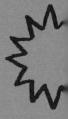

## 2.

# Protest, Resist, Rage

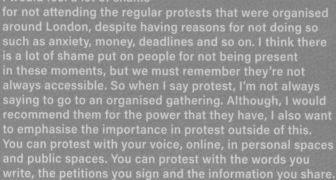

You don't have to attend a protest in order to protest. I would feel a lot of shame for not attending the regular protests that were organised around London, despite having reasons for not doing so such as anxiety, money, deadlines and so on. I think there is a lot of shame put on people for not being present in these moments, but we must remember they're not always accessible. So when I say protest, I'm not always saying to go to an organised gathering. Although, I would recommend them for the power that they have, I also want to emphasise the importance in protest outside of this. You can protest with your voice, online, in personal spaces and public spaces. You can protest with the words you write, the petitions you sign and the information you share.

The temptation to allow things to pass you by should be resisted when possible. When Priti Karen Patel tries to pass another bill that furthers to silence us, resist it. Don't allow things to happen just because 'so many things are happening'. It's difficult and balance it against your life. Empathy should allow to flow freely to manage these moments in the time you have. There's no expectation for you to be sitting at a keyboard, furiously signing every petition made. There's an expectation that when you can and have the ability to, you resist against the system.

Trying not to type Rage Against The Machine, but there it is. I just did it. I grew up listening to them and I loved everything about their messages. Saw them perform at Reading Festival and it was a holy moment. Anyway, this isn't about the band. You're allowed to be angry in these moments of protest and resistance. Your emotions are valid and so are your concerns. If being angry makes others uncomfortable, maybe they need to join your level of emotion instead of attempting to downplay it. Your anger is powerful and necessary.

✳✳✳✳✳✳✳✳✳✳✳✳✳✳✳✳✳✳✳✳✳✳✳✳✳✳✳✳✳

# 3.

# Learn Then Educate

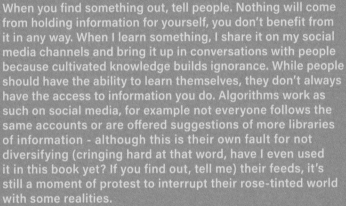

When you find something out, tell people. Nothing will come from holding information for yourself, you don't benefit from it in any way. When I learn something, I share it on my social media channels and bring it up in conversations with people because cultivated knowledge builds ignorance. While people should have the ability to learn themselves, they don't always have the access to information you do. Algorithms work as such on social media, for example not everyone follows the same accounts or are offered suggestions of more libraries of information - although this is their own fault for not diversifying (cringing hard at that word, have I even used it in this book yet? If you find out, tell me) their feeds, it's still a moment of protest to interrupt their rose-tinted world with some realities.

Usually when I mention something I learn myself, the wide-eyed recipient is thankful for this and eager to pass it forward. If they share things on their social media, it will reach more people who aren't within your own bubbles of activism. Sometimes, people aren't thankful and that's their prerogative. They can choose to be ignorant, but you have done what you can on a social media platform.

Outside of social media, if you have access to platforms, speak about injustices that you are aware of. I want to pause here and remind people that this activism is within a person's ability. A lot of people are unable to speak up and when we (some Asians for example) have privilege, we should attempt to clear harm's way for Black people. Don't expect your Black or Asian friend to keep telling you about injustice either. This work is hard, draining and almost impossible to keep up with. These points are here to remind you of what you can do as a PoC, but it's also for white people to notice this pain and step up.

## 4.

# Question It All

When something uncomfortable happens, question where it came from. There have been far too many times that I've put something down to individual preference or coincidence, when it clearly is about race, gender or sexuality. When someone puts you in an uncomfortable place, encourage yourself to ask where the discomfort comes from. Is there trauma about your very existence in there somewhere? Are you questioning parts of yourself because of it? More times than none, the microaggressions of racism, sexism, homophobia, transphobia and ableism leads to your pain. If you spot it, call it out. No one should feel they have a priority of comfort. And no one should especially continue the cycle of pain they have inflicted on you onto others. People will definitely say 'they always say it's because of their race, you can't do anything around them!'

And you know, that's interesting to me, because when people say they are walking on eggshells around you, it's strange they complain since they put the eggs there themselves. Why would you surround yourself with eggs? You're not irrational. Someone else has done that, so they don't have to broach certain subjects. When they start complaining about all these annoying eggshells they're stepping on, that's actually a good thing. They are finally dealing with the aggressions they surrounded you with.

Them: 'I feel like I'm walking on eggshells around you!'
You: 'Thank you for dealing with the trauma'

## 5.
# Don't Stop

It's not a trend. It's not a hashtag. When it doesn't affect you directly, you can ignore it most of the time, but those who it affects will never be able to forget. When you're in a position of power or privilege, you're able to make some change. Simply by normalising certain things such as oh I don't know, that Black lives matter and always do. Don't stop there. Black trans lives matter too. Speak about it.

I don't for one moment expect the entire world to organise all at once, all with enough accessibility and privilege to be part of a conversation. I want people to take a break and to spend time with people they love and who love them. I want people to feel empathy grow inside them while they go about their day. What I don't want is for selective and performative activism based around social cues.

When the informative Instagram posts stop circulating, it doesn't mean your activism can stop. When everyone paused from posting on Instagram in the summer of 2020, during large anti-racism protests, then eventually continued their brand of beige, with no comment on what was happening – it was loud. The echo of the silence was heard. While some people say 'we don't post much' or 'we don't use social media' or 'we do other things you can't see' that's fine, go ahead and do that and please don't stop doing that. But remember, it's difficult to feel comfortable around people unless they have positioned themselves as people who won't roll their eyes at conversations about race. It's not a question of the amount of engagement you get on social media, it's about us, looking at you and wondering if you're safe.

'Do we need a sign or something, god!' – I hear you.

Our sign is our skin, our partners, our trauma, our histories. Wear yours on your skin. Wear yours proudly.

187

Hold Them To Account

\*\*\*\*\*\*\*\*\*\*\*\*\*\*\*\*\*\*\*\*\*\*\*\*\*\*\*\*\*\*\*\*\*\*

xamining why things are bounced between different generations and where they originate from help us to decipher how to make that change within ourselves and in turn, how we view the world. As Zarina said to me on the phone 'the average Steve off the street won't know the nuance of racism, if you ask him how to get rid of it, he'll say "um just don't do it". He won't say that we need to decriminalise drugs or abolish prisons.' So we have to thrive to not be average Steve off the street. Average Steve is the reason we're still here, the reason this book has been published (I guess thanks Steve?), and the reason why our humanity thrives on injustice.

I spoke about empathy to a friend recently, and how I feel a lot of us lack the ability to empathise with anyone other than our immediate people. What we do is see those around us as individual people and strip them of their status in society. For example, I'm Sharan – not queer British Indian woman. And that's great, I don't want anyone near me who only sees me as that. But while you see me as that person who is obsessed with horror films and is also terrified of the dark but will still make you watch all the new releases with her, so you text her when a new film comes out ... the empathy you have is you should reach out to me when my intersects cause trauma too. When you see something homophobic happening, know that inside me something is crushed. When something racist happens, my internal struggle is shrouded in an intense pain. When gendered violence puts white women to the forefront and women of colour, specifically Black women are ignored – I notice.

Empathy should allow you to feel the source of pain across the world, because as it effects those around you, it will eventually transmit back to you. It currently doesn't allow for that. The main culprit is the ignorance in understanding – whether it's through research, listening, speaking, attending, observing, silently understanding the part of the world you can ignore. While people don't have access to learning resources to be able to 'read up' on histories (poverty, learning difficulties, disabilities, time, land, space ...), people can still listen when they have the ability to, and with this silence comes empathy.

Alright, enough of that mushy stuff.

The words that really stick out to me in this book (other than ass) are 'dirty' and 'disgusting'. They are used to describe women and non-binary people, especially queer and poor people. They are used to describe darker skin tones, hairy people and people who are sexually liberated. These words are etched into our skin as a reminder that we are not good enough. Through a history of racist hair removal practices to the Mughal Empire dated caste system, people are listed in a pyramid scheme hierarchy and considered expendable.

Our bodies have been gifted through from ancestors – sharp multilingual tongues, dark hair flowing down our backs like rivers, brown eyes that hold a history of centuries of art and the dark circles painted around our eyes that portray the weight of these histories being demolished. We must hold these parts of us with pride. We are bearing the weight of our beautiful history in our bodies and instead of seeing it as a curse, we must acknowledge the gift of it. When we feel the weight of it all too heavy, it's because of the heaviness of oppression. With it, we can fall to our knees, but we won't topple.

It's not for us to have to get the oppression off our backs. But unfortunately, we have to do a lot of the work because colonisers don't leave your land or pay reparations. But we shouldn't have to and it's unfair to expect us to. It's unfair to have to write a whole book listing out trauma for people to understand why whiteness is violent. It's unfair that despite our history, present and future, we are still just 'using the race card' instead of asking for help to remove some of the weight off our backs.

There's little we can do about white supremacy and colonial history, other than learn how it affects us and how we equip the knowledge to enact change. Ideally I would like to see all power structures fall, like a slow motion video of a building being demolished, but the reality is far from that. Why would those who hold power decide to let go of it? They greedily grab at power and shove it into their pockets. I guess we should learn how to pickpocket.

I will never stop saying this: your words inspire, but your actions define you. •

# Our Bodies Have Been Gifted from

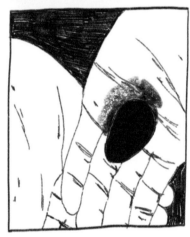

# our Ancestors

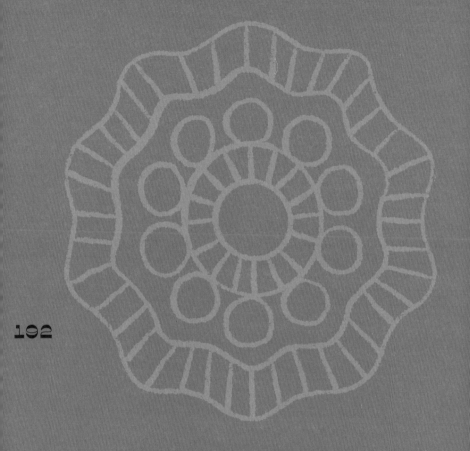

# I am Sharan Dhaliwal, and I approve this message

While, as you have witnessed, I can talk for far too long about far too many things, there are people out there who I regularly learn from, am inspired by and help me understand the world that little bit more to allow for my own research. I won't keep them from you, in order to be able to make movements, I want everyone to be open to the conversations I have.

# Books

**Why I'm No Longer Talking To White People About Race** by Reni Eddo-Lodge
Bloomsbury Publishing (2018)

**Brit(ish): On Race, Identity and Belonging** by Afua Hirsch
Vintage (2018)

**White Tears / Brown Scars: How White Feminism Betrays Women of Color** by Ruby Hamad
Trapeze (2020)

**What White People Can Do Next: From Allyship to Coalition** by Emma Dabiri
Penguin (2021)

**The Wretched of the Earth** by Frantz Fanon
Penguin Classics (2001)

**Girl, Woman, Other** by Bernardine Evaristo
Penguin (2020)

**The Good Immigrant** edited by Nikesh Shukla
Unbound (2017)

**It's Not About The Burqa** edited by Mairiam Khan
Picador (2020)

**The Clapback: Your Guide to Calling out Racist Stereotypes** by Elijah Lawal
Hodder & Stoughton (2019)

**Insurgent Empire: Anticolonialism and the Making of British Dissent: Anticolonial Resistance and British Dissent** by Priyamavada Gopal
Verso (2020)

# Podcasts

### About Race
### by Reni Eddo-Lodge

### Black Gals Livin'
### by Victoria Sanusi and Jasmine Braithwaite

### Code Switch
### by NPR

### Growing up with gal-dem
### by gal-dem magazine

### Brown Baby
### by Nikesh Shukla

I probably shouldn't be saying this but read *Burnt Roti*! The magazine is full of amazing essays and interviews with phenomenal South Asian people. Not only will it widen your understanding on some marginalised groups, it will also make you aware of cool shows out there, interesting movements and global political issues. Every single person who has spent time and energy to contribute to the magazine, those who have sent me an email and waited forever for me to reply, because my inbox looks like Charlie in the mailroom in *It's Always Sunny* ... and everyone who has supported the work – you are what has made *Burnt Roti*. All I do is reap the rewards of your work. I get yelled at for saying stuff like that, so sure, I put a lot of time and energy into managing the platform and moving conversations forward, but I would be nothing without you all. So, if you want to understand more about South Asian identity, diaspora, art, theatre, politics ... you'll see some of it shine on our website and in our print magazine.

And in this book, you will find interviews by beautiful people, who gave me their time and energy. For those who aren't anonymised, you should search them and their work. Learn from them, just like I have. I've only given you a small snippet of their brains. Go dig deeper.

Either from researching the suggestions above, or any other media you come across, I hope this book has helped with your journey in some way. Conversations about whiteness, supremacy, privilege and fetishization have been had for decades now – I'm not saying anything new. But I'm also aware that the crossover of queer, British and Indian has been greatly lacking. Not because we're so few or submissive in our abilities, but because we haven't been given the chance. I hold onto the privilege I have been given to speak my mind, because it is rarely afforded.

We covered a lot here and some of it may be hard to read. Whether it's from disordered eating or light skin privilege, there's a lot here to make some of us feel uncomfortable. This discomfort for those in privilege is a long time coming. Instead of feeling a permanent discomfort, like a pulled muscle that never heals, I pass this onto someone who has never considered that my muscles ache because of everything I carry. And for those who carry a lot too, this book will lift some of that weight because we don't carry it individually.

**This is collective.**

**Collective pain,**

**collective joy,**

**collective relief.**

198

# Sharan Dhaliwal, Writer

Sharan Dhaliwal founded, developed and now runs the UK's leading South Asian culture magazine *Burnt Roti* – a platform for young creatives to showcase their talent, find safe spaces and destigmatise topics around mental health and sexuality. Her particular interests focus on the representations of young women, South Asian women and queer women.

Storytelling and creativity were a big part of Sharan's escapism – from books and comics to music, she would immerse herself in these worlds. She went from tracing *X-Men* characters into the back of textbooks, to writing short stories in her teens, but it wasn't until her 30s that she found her voice, writing for publications such as the *Guardian*, *Huffpost* and *i-D*. *Burnt Roti* was created out of her need to tell important stories.

Sharan grew up in Hounslow and Southall and as a queer woman felt unsafe to be herself. This led her to create Middlesex Pride – a couple years after coming out in an article in *Burnt Roti*. The pride event is for a largely immigrant community in the Greater London area to help them understand all genders and sexual preferences. She also runs Oh Queer Cupid, a monthly queer speed dating and comedy night in London. In 2019, she was on the list of global influential women for the BBC 100 Women, for the work she does with *Burnt Roti*.

This work has been a big part of her and there's something in her that wants a quiet family life. Difficult for someone who can't stop talking, but we'll see.

insta: @burntrotimag; @ sharandhaliwal_

# Aleesha Nandhra,
# Illustrator

Aleesha is an Illustrator and sometimes Printmaker from London. Since graduating from the Cambridge School of Art she has created work for the likes of Google, *The LA Times*, The Barbican and been shortlisted for The World Illustration Awards (2018).

Thematically she is drawn to work that deals with: nature, culture, mental health, music and everyday life. Narratives and visual storytelling play a huge part in her creative practice both within and away from commercial illustration. She enjoys the challenge of finding that balance between the mundane and poetic to create something evocative.

Aleesha also co-runs 'Mil Ke Chai' an artist-led café which aims to create spaces that nurture friendship and enterprise across class, caste and religion. Collaboration, community projects and creative education are all also very important to Aleesha and these feed back into her work and process.

website: www.aleeshanandhra.com, insta: @aleesha_n

## Lisa Rahman,
## Design Director

Lisa Rahman is an award-winning Creative with over 13 years industry experience. She graduated from Chelsea College of Art in 2008 and soon after started her career as an Art Intern at British *ELLE*. Her passion for print and mixed-media approach to Graphic Design was recognised by Editors early in her career and she was soon appointed Art Director of the award-winning *ELLE Collections* and went on to lead the art department at *Conde Nast*, British *Glamour* (Her multiple industry awards include: DANDAD, SPD, BSME).

In 2018 she made the leap to freelance, submerging herself in different communities of creative thinkers to continuously re-imagine the future of storytelling. She sites *Burning My Roti* as an extremely rare opportunity in her publishing career, where you get to work with so many incredible South Asians across all disciplines. She continues to build on her individual arts practice that spans commercial and editorial work whilst working on projects with a focus on community, mentorship and bridging the diversity gap in the creative industries.

website: www.lisarahman.com, insta: @lisrah

## Kajal Mistry,
## Publishing Direcor

Kajal Mistry is the Publishing Director of Hardie Grant Books London, an independent creative publishing house that specialises in illustrated non-fiction books for adults. She has worked in the publishing industry for more than 10 years. Kajal grew up in west London, in a fairly traditional Gujarati household. Homelife was always busy, with lots of family socials and events, and an endless supply of food.

From a young age, Kajal was always encouraged to read and to be creative – especially by her mother. As a child, Kajal had big ambitions to be a TV presenter (a Blue Peter presenter, to be precise), aware of the lack of South Asian representation on mainstream TV. However, after Konnie Huq got the gig (!) that dream fizzled away, and it was the publishing industry that caught her attention.

Kajal started out her publishing career as a PA at one of the world's leading global publishers and slowly, but surely, managed to work her way up through sheer determination, persistence, hard work and a sharp eye for trends. Now, as Publishing Director, Kajal is keen to explore different ideas, new ways of thinking and champion diverse voices in all subject areas, and to create a list that feels progressive, inspirational and dynamic.

Insta: @ kj_mistry

# Acknowledgements

I would like to thank an endless amount of people for this book. A lot of them are in the book themselves, who have inspired me and kept me on my toes. My agent Abi Fellows, who has always had my back through the thick and thin; helped me at my lowest and supported me at my highest. My family – many of whom didn't really understand what I'm doing here, but were excited about the book nonetheless. My friends who kept saying 'Sharan, you're writing a book, it's amazing. Now stop moaning'. To the Artist, Aleesha Nandhra and the Design Director, Lisa Rahman, whose unique collaboration made the book more than I could ever have imagined – you have translated my words into visuals perfectly, I thank you for the hard work you've put into creating this beautiful book. The publisher, Kajal Mistry at Hardie Grant, for your enthusiasm, for believing in my words and pushing me further with them. Thank you to the copy editor Amrit Matharu for reminding me celebrate myself. This team of South Asian women are important to me. Thank you to The Love of my Life for showing me the biggest ups and downs of my romantic life so far, helping me realise what love truly is. Even the bad parts. Especially the bad parts. Thank you for supporting me despite everything. Every women and non-binary people of colour who has been a part of my journey and allowed me to be part of theirs. Thank you to every person who has spoken their truth. I speak mine in your footsteps. To the people who stop me at events, in the street, at random bars to tell me they love what I do. You will never know what it means to me. I isolate myself – dissociate from my work when I'm creating. Sometimes I forget people are listening. Thank you for reminding me that everything has been worthwhile. Thank you to every queer, trans, non-binary, Black, indigenous, Asian and disabled person for the hard work they have put in. Thank you to my many therapists. Thank you.

'Thank you to every person who has spoken their truth. I speak mine in your footsteps.'

**Sharan Dhaliwal**

# For those who can't Google

### Nani
*Pronounced naan-ee*

A maternal grandma.
Tends to love gossip
and making enough food
for an entire village.

### Tava
*Pronounced tha-vah*

A flat iron skillet where
you cook your roti.

### Manjai
*Pronounced mun-jay*

Wooden framed bed, usually
kept outside for lounging
and sleeping. Also known
as charpai. Have seen
them being marketed and
resold by white people
for hundreds of pounds.
Couldn't stop laughing.

### Cha
*Pronounced cha*

Sweet masala tea, which
I didn't realise you all
meant when you were
saying 'chai', because I've
never said that in my life.
Only once while ordering
a chai latte. Hated myself
a sufficient amount after.

### TERF
*Trans Exclusionary
Radical Feminist*

A proclaimed feminist who
doesn't allow trans rights
in their ideologies. They
are very harmful people
to the trans community,
as they perpetuate myths
and false information.

## Masi

*Pronounced ma-see*

Your maternal aunt, who is somehow funnier, far more interesting, and more progressive than your own mother.

## SWERF

*Sex Worker Exclusionary Radical Feminist*

A proclaimed feminist who doesn't believe in the rights for sex workers. Consented and salaried sex work, with the worker in control, isn't considered or believed to be 'feminist' by these people.

## Besharam

*Pronounced bey-shrum*

Someone who is shameless. Basically, me.

## Ladoo

*Pronounced ludd-oo*

Indian sweet, made mostly out of sugar and in the shape of a ball. Can be bright orange or bright yellow.

205

# Notes

# Notes

Published in 2022 by Hardie Grant Books,
an imprint of Hardie Grant Publishing

Hardie Grant Books (London)
5th & 6th Floors
52–54 Southwark Street
London SE1 1UN

Hardie Grant Books (Melbourne)
Building 1, 658 Church Street
Richmond, Victoria 3121

hardiegrantbooks.com

British Library Cataloguing-in-Publication Data. A
catalogue record for this book is available from the British
Library.

Burning My Roti
ISBN: 978-178488-439-0

10 9 8 7 6 5 4 3 2 1

Publishing Director: Kajal Mistry
Copy Editor: Amrit Matharu
Proofread and Sensitivity Read: Hamza Jahanzeb
Design and Art Direction: Lisa Rahman
Illustrator: Aleesha Nandhra
Author photo on inside back cover © Kiran Gidda
Production Controller: Sabeena Atchia

Colour reproduction by p2d
Printed and bound in China by Leo Paper Products Ltd.